RAISING BACKYARD CHICKENS FOR BEGINNERS

THE EASIEST WAY TO RAISE HAPPY, HEALTHY HENS AND HAVE FRESH ORGANIC EGGS FOR LIFE

© **Copyright EcoPug Publication 2023 - All rights reserved.**

The content contained within this book may not be reproduced, duplicated or transmitted without direct written permission from the author or the publisher.

Under no circumstances will any blame or legal responsibility be held against the publisher, or author, for any damages, reparation, or monetary loss due to the information contained within this book. Either directly or indirectly. You are responsible for your own choices, actions, and results.

Legal Notice:

This book is copyright protected. This book is only for personal use. You cannot amend, distribute, sell, use, quote or paraphrase any part, or the content within this book, without the consent of the author or publisher.

Disclaimer Notice:

Please note the information contained within this document is for educational and entertainment purposes only. All effort has been executed to present accurate, up-to-date, and reliable, complete information. No warranties of any kind are declared or implied. Readers acknowledge that the author is not engaging in the rendering of legal, financial, medical or professional advice. The content within this book has been derived from various sources. Please consult a licensed professional before attempting any techniques outlined in this book.

By reading this document, the reader agrees that under no circumstances is the author responsible for any losses, direct or indirect, which are incurred as a result of the use of the information contained within this document, including, but not limited to, — errors, omissions, or inaccuracies.

Contents

Introduction	IV
1. Why Raise Backyard Chickens?	1
2. What to Consider Before Buying Chickens?	14
3. The Chicken Coop Is Where It All Begins	31
4. Choosing Your Chicken Breeds	45
5. Bringing Your Chicks Home	66
6. Providing Nutrition and Water	72
7. Laying Hen Management	87
8. Chicken Eggs: How to Collect and Clean Them?	109
9. The Most Frequent Chicken Health Issues	113
10. Protecting Chickens from Cold and Predators	133
11. Chicken Care Routine	141
12. Chicken Behavior and Psychology	146
Conclusion	152
Resources	154

INTRODUCTION

"The primary reason I started keeping chickens was for the eggs, but as time went on, I found that I really enjoyed caring for them and learning about all the different kinds of chickens that exist."

Martha Stewart

In 2020, it was estimated that around 518.3 million chickens reside in the United States. If you are reading this, then you are privileged. You have just taken the initial step in researching the requirements for raising chickens. This book seeks to provide you with the information you need to effectively care for and grow your own chickens. If you can satisfy the chickens' basic needs, they will provide you with an abundance of tasty eggs. You must be practical when acquiring chickens. Animals cannot be discarded if you decide you no longer want them. Living with chickens opens one's eyes. They are not as thoughtless as they are frequently painted to be. You will learn that they have good memories, are smart, can work as a team, have their own language, and can tell the difference between themselves and about a hundred other chickens and people.

As children, numerous of us were fascinated by dinosaurs. You may not realize that chickens and dinosaurs are closely linked. In 2018, the DNA of an extinct Tyrannosaurus was compared to the DNA of 21 animal species. The closest resemblance was to a chicken! It may come as a surprise that chickens are closely related to dinosaurs, but think of them as third cousins of the T-Rex, separated by more than 100 million years. Putting aside the compelling dinosaur connection, chickens have become the most popular backyard hobby or business over the past few decades.

Each year, tens of thousands of individuals acquire and care for our feathered companions. Keeping chickens in your backyard is not new, and at one point in our history, it was extremely prevalent. Keeping backyard chickens was promoted during the Great Depression because the food was insufficient. Families with backyard chickens had access to fresh eggs and were able to raise their own meat birds. After this time, small mom-and-pop grocery stores opened up on every corner. They sold clean, white eggs and freshly roasted chickens, so people no longer had to raise their own chickens.

The resurgence of the backyard chicken movement can be credited to a younger population interested in the green movement, the ability to manage how their animals are fed and cared for, and the enjoyment of rearing their own animals. If you have never had the pleasure of spending time with chickens, you have been deprived. Chickens have distinct personalities, and once people understand how unique they are, they often adopt them as pets and give them affectionate names that reflect their activities and characteristics. Chickens have a wonderful way of working their way into the lives of people who had never given them a second thought, regardless of what sparked their first interest. Even if you have no interest in or experience with birds, you will undoubtedly wonder how you ever survived without them at some point!

If you are familiar with merely 1% of the American food industry, you undoubtedly already know that our food might be poisoned. Industrial farmers raise animals for profit by rapidly fattening them to the maximum extent possible. To accomplish this, the animals are fed antibiotics, hormones, and synthetic compounds that accelerate their growth. In this essential book for everyone who takes their health and well-being seriously, you will discover how to grow chickens in your backyard, enjoy fresh eggs every day, and enhance your health by hundreds of percentage points.

In recent years, backyard chicken rearing has never been more popular. This is mostly due to a growing interest in self-sufficiency and locally obtained food. People tend to spend more time at home and prefer to have an organic and simpler way of life. In fact, spending time with your chickens is comparable to yoga, Pilates, and farmers' markets, in terms of quality pastimes. Surprisingly, you don't even need a vast space to keep a small flock of six egg-laying chickens. You will also discover that there is an entire business devoted to meeting your demands. There are chicken coops available to fit various spaces and budgets.

Once you have begun this path, there are numerous considerations and details to bear in mind. The purpose of this book is to make your chicken journey a little bit easier, given your hectic schedule. You'll be able to spend more time with your chickens and have fresh eggs delivered to your door every day. In addition, it will guarantee the well-being of your flock. To help you keep track of all of this important data and information, I made a set of checklists and trackers, tips and techniques, and journaling space.

Why raise chickens? Simple: fresh eggs. Having your own flock, though, can provide you with so much more. They can aid in the control of pests and weeds in the garden. Their droppings can be composted for use as fertilizer. When you observe their activities as they peck, hop, and saunter about, they may also be wonderful companions.

The following chapters contain a wealth of information on how to raise your own chickens, as well as some additional advice to assist you in avoiding making rookie mistakes. You will be able to absorb a vast array of information contained in this single book. You won't have to worry about your flock because you'll be able to see how well it does right away.

Beginning with which chickens to select and how to prepare a home for them, this book details every stage of the procedure. You will discover how to ensure their health and safety via diet, routine, and care. You will gain an appreciation for these magnificent creatures, from the chicken to the egg. You'll also learn a lot about how chickens think and interact with each other in the process.

One of the benefits of raising backyard chickens is that you don't have to get everything done in one go. Everything you do will occur in predetermined stages. Before moving on to the next step, a process usually has to be completed in its entirety. Permit me to give you a quick rundown of each one. You don't need to be a chicken; you simply need a few pointers to get started!

Keeping chickens is simple and rewarding, and you can do so just as readily in an urban yard as in a rural one. As with any other pet (cat, dog, or rabbit), you will need to provide daily care for your chickens. You must ensure that the chickens are well cared for while you are away. This book about chickens is unlike any other currently available.

Finding the information you're looking for couldn't be easier, thanks to this book's layout. Go ahead and navigate the book on your own to get a sense of how it works. If you need a quick answer, you don't need to read the full text because the headings direct your attention to the specific section you'll need. This book provides a complete review of all areas of chicken husbandry.

It is possible to get fresh eggs, amusement, and even meat from a flock of chickens in your own backyard. This book will address keeping chickens for their nutritious eggs. Just like any other animal, chickens make excellent pets. They are low-maintenance and give us a wide range of perks that other pets do not. As far as caring for them goes, you won't have to do anything but watch over them. You may like spending time with your chickens, but it's not a must like it is with dogs or other animals. As long as you provide them with food, water, and a clean environment, your family will enjoy a steady supply of fresh eggs for many years.

These advantages have made urban chickens a popular choice for homeowners. In addition, they require less room. A proper house for them, known as a coop, can be constructed or purchased with relative ease. To guarantee that your chickens are comfortable, healthy, and safe from predators, you will need a chicken coop that is sturdy and efficient. It does not need to be very specialized; in fact, the majority of people would rather make it themselves than purchase a prefabricated or kit version. This is a more budget-friendly choice that also allows for greater personalization. We will discuss chicken coops in greater depth in a later chapter.

Having backyard chickens eliminates the need to discard leftover food items. Chickens have a voracious appetite and consume nearly everything. They will consume all the ants, worms, and other small insects that might otherwise invade your home or garden. Even though chickens will eat nearly anything, you must supplement their diet with commercial feeds that contain the proper amounts of nutrients. For instance, an egg-laying chicken will require enough calcium intake. Additionally, broilers and roosters will require specific types of feed.

But aside from their feed, chickens will eat anything from fresh grass to worms, so don't limit their natural instinct to foraging and roaming in search of food. Kitchen scraps will be very beneficial for them. You must also provide them with clean water at all times. In a subsequent chapter, we will also examine feeding in greater detail. This book will cover all of the above material and much more. At the conclusion of this reading, you will have more than enough information to begin keeping your own backyard chickens. And along the way, you'll find that it is enjoyable, thrilling, and healthful!"

This book is the result of years of hands-on experience with backyard chicken raising. It is intended to be a simple and uncomplicated read. It provides the fundamentals without limiting your ability to pursue further information and projects in the future. It is a comprehensive resource that eliminates the need for cross-references. You can read it in a single sitting, but you may also refer to it multiple times throughout your project's execution.

In addition to being therapeutic, lucrative, and enjoyable, raising chickens may be somewhat nerve-wracking for novices. There is a vast amount of knowledge regarding rearing chicks and hens, making it difficult to decide what is correct, incorrect, or just plain strange. In this comprehensive guidebook, I have included all you need to know to care for your birds, from the chick to the adult chicken. Believe me when I say that once you have chickens, you will never stop learning or smiling. I have attempted to simplify it so that it does not become confusing for you. You are welcome to read and pose questions.

If you're considering raising chickens, you're in for an exciting journey! However, poultry ownership should not be treated lightly. As the caretaker of a small backyard flock, you must comprehend the dietary requirements of your flock at various points in its life. You will be responsible for your pets' medical care and treatment. You must ensure their protection from predators. Their lives will depend on you. If you take good care of them, they will prosper and live happy lives. If you do nothing, they will have to undergo a great deal of agony and suffering. I hope you'll adopt chicks with the same care as you would a dog or cat. They both deserve and require the same level of care. They will lavish you with love, attention, and affection in exchange for the comfortable lifestyle you give. This book was designed with you in mind as a toolkit for happy individuals and flocks alike. Are you all set?

Let's get going!

1

WHY RAISE BACKYARD CHICKENS?

The Benefits of Keeping Chickens

Eggs

Your hardworking backyard chickens will each produce nearly one egg a day. Golden Comet hens, for example, are bred to lay eggs and will produce 5 eggs weekly. Does anything beat the smell of freshly laid eggs in your own backyard in the morning? These eggs aren't just packed with vitamins and minerals; they also include iodine and vitamin D. Eggs from free-range hens are significantly more nutritious than those from hens maintained in less-than-ideal conditions. To get the best nutrition from an egg, you need to provide it with the best possible food for your chickens: quality chicken feed that isn't made from corn or soy.

Chicken Television

The best way to unwind is to observe the flock as they patrol the yard.

With so much going on, it's impossible to get bored:

Petty squabbles/ Interactions with one another/ Preening/ Dust baths

Spending time with your flock is a worthwhile investment because you can learn so much about their dynamics by watching them interact with one another. Over time, you may even believe they are expressing something you can understand. As a bonus, we tend to forget about our own challenges. What could be better than laughing and smiling at the sight of chickens?

Education

Knowing what you're eating and where it comes from is critical. Nowadays, many people do not know where their food comes from, how it is prepared, or even what meat actually looks like when it is alive. Children can learn a lot about animal welfare by keeping hens, hatching eggs, and taking care of baby chicks. As a parent, it's a good idea to let your kids help you care for the chickens and gather their eggs. It doesn't matter what your child's age is! Make sure to supervise youngsters as they handle the delicate chicks.

Sustainable Living

We've learned a lot in the past few years about how vulnerable our food systems are. Almost every country in the world has experienced food and commodity shortages. Many people have started rearing chickens for the first time in the last year. As far as fundamental food security is concerned, chickens can go a long way. Many households rely on them for both their meat and their eggs. Keeping a small flock of chickens in a small location can help alleviate some of the stress of food shortages. Chickens are a terrific way to get started on the path to becoming more self-sufficient. Once they're in their coop, they don't need much in the way of daily attention. As a side note, the environmental impact of food miles can be discussed here. Food that must be moved from one place to another has a high carbon impact. You can reduce your environmental footprint by raising your own chickens. It doesn't matter how small your contribution is; even a few bits can make a difference.

Quality Nutrition

If you keep your chickens for eggs or meat, you will know exactly what they consume and how healthy their living conditions are. Organic, non-GMO, or conventional feed are all options for feeding your chickens. Despite the use of terms such as "organic," "free-range," and "barn-reared," the reality of the "industrial hen" may differ greatly from our perception. No one knows exactly what the law says about poultry being reared in a yard on grass. But that's probably not how it works in practice. Eggs produced by caged chickens are less nutritious than those produced by free-roaming birds. The color, flavor, and nutritional value of an egg from a pasture-raised chicken are all enhanced by free-range farming.

Pest Control

Pests are no match for most chickens. Chickens' favorite pastime is scouting the garden for delectable bugs to add to their diet. Your flock will benefit from the extra protein provided by insects. Ticks, mosquitoes, caterpillars, and flies are just a few of the insects that chickens love to feast on. So, as a bonus, chickens are eradicating disease-carrying pests from the landscape! Chickens are known to prey on mice and snakes that happen to be in their path. Don't use poison on these rats to avoid a bloodbath. It is possible that your chickens could eat poison, even though some rat poisons are dosed quite precisely these days.

Fertilizer

People who own chickens know that their manure is a lot to deal with. The nitrogen, phosphorus, and potassium in this manure can be used to fertilize your plants. The soil requires all of these ingredients. Just keep in mind that you can't use it right away; it needs to mature first. Allow it to "cook" for a while with some fallen leaves, old straw bedding, and green yard compost. Make sure to turn it every now and then, and you'll have fantastic new soil for your garden in no time.

Factory Farming

Many people find factory farming to be unattractive, even if they don't realize it. Unfortunately, there is a great deal of gray area in the legislation that governs the handling of farm animals. Not surprisingly, factory farming has a negative impact on the environment as well. Despite the fact that considerable efforts have been made to improve the well-being of these animals, much work remains. You can treat your chickens humanely if you raise them yourself.

Reduced Waste

As omnivores, chickens can consume both meat and veggies. If you've ever raised chickens in your backyard, you know they'll eat just about anything you put in front of them. Even though they are happy to eat your leftovers, avoid giving them things like pizza or other carbohydrates too frequently. Spaghetti, peas, and maize are just some of the foods that chickens enjoy. To prevent vermin or predators from entering the coop, make sure to clean up after your chickens have finished eating.

Low-Maintenance

Your chickens are surprisingly low-maintenance once you get everything set up. Their food and water are already provided, and they don't need to be kept occupied for long periods of time. They should be allowed to go outside during the day and kept inside at night. Having an automatic chicken coop door is a good way to cut down on the amount of time you spend in the coop. Most people spend some time with them in the morning or during the day. Despite their low upkeep, the great majority of people like going out with their flock. This is a fantastic time to make sure that your chickens are getting enough food and water, as well as to gather their lovely eggs.

Therapy

Yes, chickens can also be used as therapy animals. Unlike therapy dogs, keeping chickens has not been well examined scientifically, although there is growing acceptance that it can be extremely beneficial for people with autism. Children benefit the most from having chickens because they give them a sense of direction, order, and self-worth. People suffering from anxiety, depression, and loneliness have found relief via the use of chicken therapy. Some people may be surprised by the employment of chickens in these domains, but chickens are actually quite intelligent and can even show signs of empathy. Their antics make it impossible not to smile while watching them go about their daily routines.

Unique Pets

Some people persist in keeping pet chickens. In comparison with a dog or cat, they have fewer things to care for, produce more income (eggs), and are quieter. The number of people keeping chickens as pets has progressively increased over the years. A pet chicken is an excellent option for people who live in apartments where pets such as cats and dogs are not permitted. In apartments and other limited settings, their small stature makes them ideal residents. They only require a few basic necessities, such as a place to sleep, a place to wash, food, and water. You may buy or make your own chicken diapers, so you'll never have any unpleasant surprises to deal with!

Breed Conservation

Some people choose to care for a small herd of rare breeds. Having a small flock of their own will provide them with eggs, which in turn will assist the breed by supplying them with eggs. If eggs aren't important to you, Sultan chickens might be a good choice because of their poor laying reputation. As always, do your research before choosing a breed to ensure it will work well for you and your lifestyle.

Social Community

It's possible to join an enormous online community once you start raising chickens. Every aspect of raising and caring for chickens is covered in these groups. They also discuss issues, including family, other pets, and more. They can assist you with issues like brooding chickens—a phrase that describes hens that want their eggs to hatch—and other chicken-related issues. In these groups, there are literally thousands of people who love talking about their chickens.

Why Keeping Chickens in Your Yard Is Not a Good Idea

Bad Eggs

Backyard chickens aren't for you if you prefer bland-tasting eggs with thin, runny whites and pale yolks. Fresher, more visually appealing, and slightly greater in nutritional content are some of the advantages of backyard chicken eggs, as opposed to the thousands of other eggs collected, graded, packed, and delivered for sale when a factory chicken lays an egg. In fact, a farmer has 30 days to do so in order to sell the eggs. After the eggs have been placed on the market, the seller has a further 30 days to sell them. When you buy fresh eggs from a farm, they could be two months old. It's easier for fresh eggs to keep their shape. You'll also note that industrial chicken yolks tend to be a darker shade of orange. The yolks of pasture-raised chicken eggs will be bright orange and stand tall. Lastly, free-range eggs are higher in antioxidants, omega-3 fatty acids, vitamins A, D, E, and B, as well as omega-6 fatty acids.

Vacations and Pet Sitters

Do you like spending time on the weekends relaxing and doing nothing? Don't get any chickens, then. They expect to be awake and active at the crack of dawn, if not earlier. An automatic chicken coop door is certainly an option, but it may be quite pricey. To properly care for any animal, even chickens, you must devote attention to it. Even your family will start to grumble if you become addicted to raising chickens. At times, you might even prefer your flock to your loved ones! Keeping chickens doesn't take a lot of time, and most daily duties can be completed in less than an hour — but they must be done. In order to take a trip without worrying about your flock, you'll need to prepare for it like a military operation. However, feeding and watering them is still a need. To keep the animals safe, they will still need to be let out in the morning and locked up at night. Finding a sitter for your chickens can be a challenge, and training them to perform the tasks you demand takes some planning ahead of time.

Neighbors and Complaints

Some neighbors love chickens, while others loathe them. Chickens may not be a good idea if your neighbors are difficult. Most of the time, you can get along with even the most annoying neighbor by giving them eggs. Your neighbor may even take care of your chickens while you're away on vacation. Even if your property is zoned for chickens, you will still need to observe local ordinances. If you don't, some of your neighbors may try to coerce you into getting rid of your flock for no good reason.

Fresh Air and Space

Roosters need a lot of room. The coop should have four square feet of space for each chicken, and the run should have eight square feet of space for each chicken as well. That allows them to freely wander around without fear of being approached or pecked at by more powerful individuals in the flock. It is also important for them to have access to natural light and fresh air. You can't keep chickens in your basement, attic, or spare room for the long term, and it's not healthy for you or your family either. It's best to keep your chickens outside in the cooler weather, unless they're birds that need a warmer climate (Sultans, Seramas, and others). If you don't have a large enough yard to keep chickens, you may want to reconsider.

Chicken Math

Chicken math, also called "more chickens" or "chicken sickness," is a disease with signs that show up over time. Once you've contracted this illness, you'll find yourself staring at chicks of all sizes, colors, and forms. To keep your partner in the dark, you'll start actively brainstorming ways to get more laying chickens than you already have. When someone asks you how many chickens you have, you'll be able to respond, "ten . . . ish." It is often referred to as "more hens disease" because you always need more chickens. Your family and friends will look at you with sympathy and shake their heads in disbelief as you struggle with this debilitating illness.

Cheap Eggs and Money

Your gorgeous free-range eggs will not be as inexpensive as you might expect. Eggs from your own backyard will be more expensive than those from the supermarket. Keeping chickens in the backyard can be pricey. It costs about $2 to buy a dozen eggs at the grocery store right now. Because these eggs are subsidized by the government, they are extremely affordable. Starting a flock is an expensive endeavor. In order to protect them from the elements, they'll need to be housed in a coop. They'll need bowls for their food and water. You'll have to spend some money upfront, but it'll be worth it in the long run.

Flower Gardens

The gardens are a chicken's playground. A well-cared-for flower or vegetable garden is their favorite. They'll try all the plants and just eat the ones they think taste good. Chickens will go to great lengths to remove mulch from flower beds, leaving behind craters in the soil. In order to have a beautiful garden and keep your hens out, you'll need to set up a fence. Set it high enough so they can't get a bird's-eye view. If you don't have fliers or bantams, a distance of 3 to 4 feet should be enough.

Knowledge

You will learn a lot when you begin to raise chickens. Providing chickens with the right food, water, and shelter is essential. First, if you plan to raise chickens for whatever reason, do some research first. What are they eating? How often do they mate? Libraries typically carry books on chicken-raising or may order them for you, and of course, the internet is an option as well. In some ways, the internet is a curse. Some sites are quite helpful and provide current information, while others perpetuate old wives' tales or simply incorrect information. Whenever you come across something that seems out of the ordinary, don't be afraid to double-check it on a different site.

Nightly Lock Up

It is imperative that you keep your chickens in an enclosed area at night for their own protection. Although it's not likely that they'll end up in trouble, foxes, raccoons, and other predators will be on the prowl. Nothing screams "dinner" like a chicken coop that is open while the chickens are snoozing. It's a full-time job to keep your flock safe from predators, but with careful preparation and attention to detail, the hazards can be minimized or eliminated. Even if you believe that your location is free of predators, it is not. You haven't seen them yet. Cities and metropolitan environments are home to foxes, raccoons, and hawks. There are far more predators in rural regions (such as fishers, bobcats, and coyotes) than in cities. Even if you don't see them, if you have chickens, they will come to investigate.

Poop and More Poop

It's no secret that chickens excrete a lot of feces. As long as you remove it every day, it's not too bad. But if you wait too long, you'll end up with some serious shoveling muscles. Another thing to think about is where you'll be disposing of the waste. Direct application of chicken manure to plants will result in plant death. You'll need to store it in a compost pile until it's old enough to use. If you don't want to deal with chicken waste, don't get chickens.

Bugs and Other Delights

Insects like mites, lice, and worms are all too common in chickens. Some effort will be required to find and treat these creatures. Giving medicine to a cat may be worse than giving a chicken a dust bath, but it has its advantages. Flies are attracted to chicken manure. There are several things you can do to limit the number of flies in your home, including keeping your ladies clean, hanging fly tape high above, and using other methods.

Sadness and Passing

Chickens, sadly, have a short lifespan. The average chicken's lifespan is eight years. Their unique characteristics will seep into yours as well, so keep an eye out for them. If you care about them, they'll eventually die, regardless of how much you love them. However, no matter how many times your friends tell you, "Well, it was only a chicken," you will still experience the pain of losing a close companion. Make sure you're prepared for a little melancholy when those particular chickens leave you, especially children.

2

WHAT TO CONSIDER BEFORE BUYING CHICKENS?

How Much Room Do Chickens Require in Their Cage?

An important consideration when starting a chicken-keeping business is how many square feet your flock will require in order to be content. When it comes to the size of your chicken house, there are several variables to take into account. How many chickens do you have? Is their growth complete? Is there going to be a run outside? Providing too much space for your chickens is preferable to providing too little. Keeping chickens in close quarters for too long can make them a little grumpy.

What Size Chicken Coop Do You Need?

If your chickens have access to the outdoors, a decent rule of thumb is 3 to 5 square feet of coop area per chicken. To be on the safe side, provide some room that is at the higher end of this size range. Depending on the size of your chicken, you'll want to follow a different set of guidelines. As long as the hens are free-roaming, they can be housed in a coop as small as 2 feet per bird. At least 3 square feet per chicken is required for medium varieties like Leghorn, while larger breeds like Plymouth Rock require at least 4 square feet.

How big of a chicken coop do you need for 10 chickens? If you have an outdoor run as well as a minimum of 3 feet per medium-sized chicken, your chicken coop will be about 30 square feet in size. If possible, plan for more. Some people propose 60 to 80 square feet for ten grown chickens or an 8×10-square-foot coop. In case of extreme weather or other reasons, the coop space will need to be significantly greater than in the instances above. Bantams, on the other hand, are so small that they require 5 square feet of space per chicken instead of the standard 2. A medium-sized breed would require 8, while a large-sized breed would require 10. Additionally, you can use online calculators to figure out how big a chicken coop should be. If you don't have a yard, a coop, or a run, some of these give various estimations based on the size of your yard.

Roosting and Running in the Outdoors

If you can, allow your hens to roam outside as much as possible. It's possible to get away with a smaller indoor chicken coop if the weather is moderate and your chickens spend most of their time outside. For each chicken, try to allocate at least 10 square feet of outside space. It's worth noting that the more space you provide your chickens, the more content they will be. Your coop should include at least 8 to 12 inches of roosting bars for each bird so they may sleep securely at night. It's possible to utilize hardwood perches or a Thermo-Chicken Perch that is heated in the winter. Every three to four chickens should have their own nesting boxes. Consider using a heated pad when it's cooler.

Chickens Necessitate a Certain Amount of Privacy

The general consensus is that a large coop is preferable to a small one. If you have the room, go for the larger coop. Why is this the case? When chickens are forced to live in cramped confines for an extended period of time, they can become a little stir-crazy. Their aggressiveness could cause feather-pulling among them. It's possible that stressed-out hens will lay fewer eggs. In most cases, too much space is preferable to too little. Make your chicken coop as large as possible in order to maximize your space. It's much better if you have the space to allow your hens to spend some time outside each day. Chickens, like humans, require a private haven of their own. Your chickens will be extremely appreciative. As a reward, you'll get a plethora of delicious eggs.

Here are a few reputable US suppliers, manufacturers, and wholesalers:

https://www.mcmurrayhatchery.com/index.html

https://www.tractorsupply.com/tsc/cms/chick-days

https://www.meyerhatchery.com/

Here are a few reputable UK suppliers, manufacturers, and wholesalers:

https://www.pipinchicksilkies.com/poultry-suppliers/

https://www.cyril-bason.co.uk/

https://charlotteschickens.co.uk/

Starting a Chicken Farm in Your Backyard: 7 Steps to Success

Step 1: Find out what the local laws and regulations are.

If you want to keep chickens in the city or suburbs, you'll need to check with your city, state, local, and homeowner's association rules before you get started. Because of the noise, roosters are prohibited in many regions, and some places limit the number of backyard chickens you can own. Some jurisdictions still outlaw the keeping of chickens. Don't get too far down the chicken path before checking the laws.

Step 2: Prepare your brooder.

Most likely, you'll be starting your flock with baby birds rather than eggs that have just been laid. Incubating and hatching eggs is a specialty for more experienced chicken keepers, so I'd hold off on trying it until you've gotten some experience with chickens. Brooders—heated enclosures used for raising baby birds—are needed because the chicks won't be with their mother hen for a long time after they hatch. In the wild, a mother hen would offer all of these things, but when we take on the role of Mama Hen, we have to step in and make them ourselves. In the classic brooding setup, a waterer, pine shavings, a large cardboard box, a feeder, and a heat lamp are used.

This is a great way to get started for a low cost. However, baby chick lungs can be damaged by pine shavings, and the heat lamp can cause your house to catch fire if you don't keep an eye on it. A cardboard or plywood box filled with corn cob bedding (which is generally used for horse stalls but can be obtained at practically any farm supply store) is a better alternative. It's inexpensive, absorbent, and gentle on the lungs of the chicken. You can use an electric radiant heat brooder in place of the heat lamp. It's a little more expensive than using a heat lamp, but there are no dangers of fire or variable temperatures.

In the same way that a mother hen raises her chicks, the brooder lamp does the same for the chicks. If you want to raise more than one litter of chicks, this is a fantastic investment—and the resale value is excellent too. The brooder must be kept safe from any potential predators, including your other pets (such as dogs, cats, and so on). Keep it away from children and pets. Brooders should be simple to clean because you'd be surprised at how much small poop chicks can make, and you'll want to keep things neat and orderly while they're growing big and strong.

Step 3: Select a breed and purchase your chicks.

Like dogs, cats, or any other animal, chickens come in a variety of breeds. Some chickens have a tendency to become agitated and flit about. Some are affectionate and cuddly. Some hens produce eggs that come in a variety of vibrant hues. There are certain chicken breeds that flourish in hot weather. Some are designed to withstand temperatures as low as −20°F. You and your family must decide on the qualities that are most important to you. I'd suggest Speckled Sussex, Light Brahmas, and Cuckoo Marans as three breeds if you're seeking a non-anxious, good-laying companion.

An internet hatchery, a farm/hardware store, or a local poultry farm are all options for purchasing chicks. In the spring, most people buy chicks from a local farm store. The choice of breeds available to you will be limited, but larger farm stores will have a wide number of options. Chicks that have been verified to be hens from birth are the best bet. If you're looking for hens, a hatchery may be your best bet, as many farm stores only sell straight-run chickens. As with anything in life, there are both advantages and disadvantages to purchasing chicks from an internet hatchery. The pros include the ability to select certain breeds, the provision of only hens, and the generally excellent health of the chicks. Due to the stress of shipping, there are several drawbacks (for both the chicks and you). If the weather gets chilly or there are shipping delays, you may lose some chicks.

Finding a local hatchery where you can pick up your chicks is the best of both worlds. If you don't want to deal with the inconvenience and stress of shipping, these retailers usually have a bigger assortment and better selection. You'd be surprised at the number of hatcheries of all sizes (especially in rural areas). Ask around at your local farmers' market or to people who sell eggs in your neighborhood. Alternatively, you can look for "hatchery" and the name of your region or town on Google.

Now that you've decided where to purchase your chicks, you must now choose the number of chicks you desire! And they're dirt cheap (you can usually find them for about $3 or $5 each). But remember that each fluffy baby chick will grow into a large, pooping, eating adult chicken, and you'll need a lot of room for them. The best approach to getting started is to get a few ladies and then expand from there. (In the future, you may always add more chickens to your flock.) You can truly give your chicks the attention they need. Once they're laying with a small group, you may expect to receive 2 to 3 eggs daily.

Step 4: Take your chicks home and care for them.

Chick care is actually rather straightforward. You must ensure that the chicks have access to clean water and high-quality starter food. In the future, the more time you spend with them, the tamer they'll become. You can certainly find the answer to your query in the thriving internet community devoted to raising backyard chickens. There is a condition known as "pasty butt" that can be caused by inconsistency in the amount of heat you receive. When using a typical heat lamp, you must wipe your chick's bum with a warm, damp paper towel at least twice daily for the first week. As long as the weather is warm enough, you can take them outside and let them walk about for a while—just make sure you have a way to keep them safe.

Step 5: Establish Permanent Housing

After around 6 weeks in the brooder, your chicks will be ready to migrate into the coop. When it comes to building your own coop, 6 weeks is the ideal amount of time! You may save a lot of money by making your own chicken coop. If you don't have the resources or time to build your own, I strongly recommend contacting your local farm store to recommend a coop for you. In addition, you may find a wide variety of creative ideas for recycled chicken coops on Pinterest! It's usually best to make a coop as large as possible. If you have a lot of space, you can always maintain fewer chickens, but if you have a small coop, it will be tough to keep many chickens. There are usually three spots in your coop where you will require bedding. Use straw in the nesting boxes, and the chickens will make nests out of it. It's just like in the brooder. You can also use sand. The primary benefits of using sand in the coop during the summer are that it keeps the coop cool and it is easy to clean (just like kitty litter).

Step 6: Make a feeding and ranging plan.

It's possible that this decision has been made for you already, as many local laws restrict backyard chickens from venturing outside of an enclosed run or coop. You'll have to make some decisions about what you feed your chickens and whether or not they're allowed to roam freely if your local rules don't require you to coop them up. However, free-range chickens are prey animals, making them difficult to protect against predators. If you're willing to accept that risk, free-ranging will provide you with the healthiest eggs, the happiest chickens, and a lower feeding expense. In between confined and free-range, the chickens can roam freely in a big run or pen during the day and then be cooped up at night for the rest of the time. You'll need to feed your chickens high-quality poultry feed, regardless of whether you choose to keep them in a coop or free-range. Free-ranging or penned-ranging your flock will only necessitate supplementing their diet because the bugs and plants they forage for will provide them with the majority of their nutritional needs. You'll be feeding them their entire diet if they're kept in a cage all the time. In either case, you're looking for high-quality products. A bird that is fed high-quality feed will produce better eggs than one that isn't, and you can taste the difference. No matter what you feed your flock, you'll need to choose a reputable supplier in your area. Peckishness is a natural reaction for chickens when their food supply is low.

Step 7: Put your chickens in their coop and watch them flourish!

Your baby chicks will need to be gradually introduced to the outdoors until the big day when they move permanently into their coop. It's a good time to do it just after they've shed all of their fluff and have a complete set of feathers to keep them warm. Your flock should be housed in their coop for approximately a week prior to going on the range. This will help the birds learn that the coop is where they belong. After that, you can release them to roost, and they'll return each night around dusk. As soon as things start to go awry, they know where to go: their safe house. Maintain a clean coop and well-fed chickens, and you should be able to collect your first egg in as little as 3 months. However, this might vary greatly depending on the breed, season, and other circumstances. On average, chickens begin laying at about 6 months of age. Chickens that are free-ranging or pen-roaming may not know how to lay eggs in a nesting box, so keep a lookout for other signs of laying, such as brilliant red combs. Locking the chickens in their coop for a week and putting phony eggs in the nesting boxes will solve the problem. So, if they observe a chicken laying in the same spot as them, it makes them more likely to follow suit. After that, the girls will continue to use their nesting boxes on a regular basis.

A Beginner's Guide to Chicken-Raising

Urban backyards around the country are becoming home to flocks of hens. Buying bins of cute peeping chicks at the feed shop might be as enticing as collecting fresh eggs from your own chickens in your own backyard. The popular sport of backyard chicken raising has many advantages, but there are some things to keep in mind first.

Verify the Laws in Your Area

If you're thinking about raising backyard chickens, the first thing you should do is check with your local government to see what the rules are in your area. All three of the following: the number of hens you can have in your coop, the number of roosters you can keep, and the distance your coop must be from your neighbor's property line are all subject to local ordinances. Check with your local government to see whether you need permission to keep chickens or if you need a building permit for a coop larger than a specific size to avoid any future issues. Changing the law is your best bet if you can't keep chickens or don't like the restrictions. You should do this before you acquire your chicks.

Breeds/Flock Sizes

It's time to do some research about the types of hens you'd like to keep in your backyard. The personalities and temperaments of different breeds vary greatly. For example, Buff Orpingtons, Cochins, and Australorps are all docile breeds that are ideal for households with children. Extreme cold or heat necessitates specific breeds. Three chickens are a nice number for a beginner flock because chickens are highly social.

Easter Egg chickens are a breed that produces colored eggs. You can buy day-old chicks online from a hatchery at your local feed store, or you can buy a range of breeds at a local feed store. Breed information can also be found on the websites of hatcheries.

Because hens are very social creatures, a flock of no fewer than three is an ideal starting point. Three laying hens should produce roughly a dozen eggs. For households with a few extra members, a henhouse with five or six chickens is a decent option.

Getting Your Chicks to Arrive at the Right Time

For the first 8 weeks of a chick's existence, it must be kept under a heat lamp in the house. They can't keep warm on their own until they develop feathers. The arrival of chicks should be timed properly so that you can move them outside as soon as possible. In order to accomplish this, you should plan to bring your chicks into the world 8 weeks before the nighttime temperatures are expected to remain above 55 degrees.

Supplies

You'll need a brooder (a cardboard box or plastic tote will do), a heat lamp, a waterer and feeder for chicks, and chick feed before your chicks arrive. Your chicks should eat chick feed until they're 8 weeks old, then switch to starter/grower feed until they're 18 weeks old, at which point they should switch to layer feed.

Chickens need a place to live. This 8-week window should give you plenty of time to gather information, choose a design, and begin construction on your own chicken coop. Additionally, there are coop kits available for purchase online or from the shed and building firms. If you're looking for a secondhand coop or shed that can be converted into a cheap coop, Craigslist is an excellent resource.

A coop with 3–5 square feet of floor area for each hen, an 8-inch roosting bar, and one nesting box for every 3–4 hens is a good idea. If you have a backyard chicken coop, an adjoining run with at least 10 square feet of room for each hen is a smart idea because predators are a concern for most backyard flocks. Three to four hens can be housed in a single nesting box.

Training Your Pets

One of the leading causes of backyard chicken deaths is the presence of domestic dogs. The reality is that if you don't train your dog to behave around your hens, you may lose them to your beloved family pet, which is something no one wants to think about. To prepare for the arrival of chicks, you should undertake some basic training with your dog, such as teaching him to drop, leave, remain, or sit.

Allow your dog to inspect the brooder when the chicks arrive and keep an eye on him near the chicks when they're there. When the hens are out of the house, put your dog on a leash and give him a firm correction if he lunges at them. Even when playing, dogs should not be permitted to chase chickens. Setting and enforcing boundaries with your dog can help him become an excellent predator deterrent and a superb flock guardian. Each hen should have 3–5 square feet of floor area and an 8-inch roosting bar in their coop.

Eggs

For the first 3 to 4 years, your backyard chickens will produce eggs at a steady rate. If you consider that a chicken can live for another 6 or more years, it's important to make long-term strategies as well.

How to Begin Raising Chickens in Simple Steps

Backyard flocking is becoming increasingly popular among American families.

Fresh, healthy eggs and the thrill of watching an egg-laying hen develop from a tiny chick to a full-fledged chicken can be yours if you have the right coop, chicks, and strategy. Create a plan before you start raising chickens in your backyard.

Set up your brooder, and get it ready to go. Each chick should have at least 2–3 square feet of floor space to roam around on for the first 6 weeks. For the first week, keep the brooder temperature at 90°F. Every week, lower the thermostat's setting by 5 degrees until it reaches 55°F.

Invest in cleanliness. Make sure your brooder is clean. Before introducing fresh chicks, make sure the area is thoroughly dry.

Educate yourself on the importance of feeding your chicks a healthy diet. New chicks require a well-balanced diet from the get-go. Layer chicks should be fed a diet that contains 18%

protein, whereas meat birds and mixed flocks should be fed a diet that contains 20% protein.

The following are six things to keep in mind before you buy baby chicks this spring:

1. Figure out what kind of chickens you want.

A wide range of poultry breeds can be found. Families are urged to use common breeds to begin raising chickens for eggs or meat. Find out what you want to get out of the flock. Consider Blue Andalusians (white eggs), Plymouth Barred Rocks (brown eggs), White Leghorn hybrids (white eggs), Rhode Island Reds (brown eggs), or Ameraucanas (blue eggs) if you want fresh eggs. Cornish Cross chickens are best suited for meat production because they grow quickly. Plymouth Barred Rock, Sussex, and Buff Orpingtons are all dual-purpose breeds that can produce both eggs and meat. For pets or displays, exotic breeds are best.

2. Determine how many birds you want.

It is possible that the number and gender of birds in your flock will be dictated by municipal restrictions and your own personal aims. Plan how much time you'll be able to spend with your flock, how much housing they'll need, how you'll gather and use eggs, and what you'll do with the birds once they stop laying eggs. Then begin with a small group of four to six chicks.

3. Choose an established source for chicks.

Buy Pullorum-Typhoid-Clean chicks from a reputable hatchery in the United States. Make sure the chicks in the hatchery are vaccinated against Marek's disease ("MD" or "fowl paralysis") and coccidiosis to avoid any potential health issues. The best place to start is by contacting your local pet supply store.

4. Set up your brooder, and get it ready to go.

A brooder is a warm, draft-free place where you can keep your newborn chicks. A heating light should be installed in the brooder, which should be totally enclosed and have a bottom surface that may be covered with bedding. The chicks will not be able to get trapped in the corner of the brooding space if the birds congregate there. At least 2 to 3 square feet of floor space is required by each chick during its first 6 weeks of life. During the first week, set the brooder temperature to 90°F, and then gradually lower the temperature by 5 degrees each week until the temperature drops to 55°F. Once the extra heat source is no longer needed, make sure you have a large, clean coop ready for the chicks. Keep a constant supply of fresh, clean water available at all times.

5. Invest in cleanliness.

Maintain a clean environment for your new chicks before they arrive and as they grow. Disinfect all materials before usage and thereafter on a weekly basis to protect the health of your young chickens. Cleansers for homes that are safe and effective are available. Don't use a disinfectant until you've read the instructions and know it doesn't leave residue behind. If the cleaner is rinsed properly after cleaning, a mixture of 10% bleach and 90% water can be effective.

6. Determine your long-term nutrition goals.

Healthy chickens are the product of strong chicks. You'll only need one starter-grower feed for the first few weeks of the hens' lives and one complete layer feed for the next few weeks thereafter. Chicks should be fed a complete starter-grower meal from the beginning. From day one, chicks need 38 different nutrients. The Purina® Oyster Strong® System is a total starter-grower diet that provides all of these nutrients. Purina® Start & Grow® or Purina® Organic Starter-Grower complete feed has an 18% protein content, making it an excellent choice for chicks who will lay eggs later in life. Choose a complete food with at least 20% protein for meat birds and mixed flocks, such as Purina® Flock Raiser® Crumbles. Chicks that are 18 to 20 weeks old should be transitioned onto a higher-calcium complete diet such as Purina® Layena®, Purina® Layena® + Omega-3, or Purina® Organic Layer Pellets or Crumbles.

3

The Chicken Coop Is Where It All Begins

The chicken coop is the first thing you should consider when thinking about raising chickens because you'll need it as soon as you get your chicks home from the breeder's facility. Here are the specifics:

Providing a Safe Haven for Your Flock

When building a chicken coop, keep these points in mind:

Shelter requirements: You'll first need a chicken coop. Water-resistant construction isn't enough for the coop; it also needs to be well-ventilated in order to remove stale, humid air while simultaneously bringing in cool, crisp air from outside. For the most part, you won't have to bother with insulating the coop in preparation for a harsh winter. Even though it's freezing outdoors, a flock of hens can make it through the winter in a coop. Heat lamps and unprotected light bulbs should never be used in chicken coops due to the constant threat of fire.

Temperature controls: Warm winters and chilly summers call for a well-ventilated chicken house. Ventilation holes should be added if you think the temperature is too high. Vents can be adjusted to keep part of the coop's warm air in during the cold winter months.

Choosing a coop: For your chickens' safety, you must provide them with a clean, dry, and well-ventilated enclosure. Your chickens require a place to sleep at night, as well as shelter from the elements. If you have enough room, you can allow your hens to roam freely, but even if you have enough room, you still need a chicken coop. Without one, eggs will be scattered all over your property, and it will be tough to find them if you don't have a coop. Your hens need to be protected from the elements and predators as well.

Chicken Coop Measurements

Chicken Types	Floor Space (birds/m^2)	Floor Space (ft^2/birds)	Perch Space (per bird)
Layer	3	3.6	25cm (10 in)
Dual-Purpose	4	2.7	20cm (8 in)
Meat	4–5	2.1–2.7	15–20cm (6-8in)

Space for Your Hens

Each of your chickens necessitates an adequate area. Chickens will develop antisocial tendencies if there isn't enough space for all of them. In the winter, everything will deteriorate to an extreme degree. When hens are bored, they get into mischief. Keeping your flock in the coop solely at night reduces the need for as much floor space as if they are pastured during the day. If your flock's more solitary individuals need a place to retreat, ensure your coop has one.

Nesting Boxes

For every three hens, you'll need approximately one box, but you can always add an extra one because more is always better. If you don't have any old grape crates or 5-gallon heaps lying around, you can always buy nesting boxes. Your hen should be able to fit comfortably in the box. Around 12 × 12 inches is a suitable size for most chickens.

Roosts

The chickens congregate on the roosts after dusk. Mostly, they prefer to sleep on the same roost or perch. One foot of perch space is required for each hen.

Fresh Air

Unless there is an absolute need, chickens should never be housed in a coop on their own. They get a kick out of running around, making a mess, and generally having a good time. If the coop is not kept clean, the air becomes stale, dusty, and might even smell like ammonia. The chickens' health can be affected by dust and ammonia. Every day, the coop should be aired to ensure the air is clean and fresh.

Protection from Predators

Your flock's safety depends on you taking security precautions. The run area, as well as the coop, must be safe. As a reminder, chicken wire will keep the chickens safe, but it will not keep predators away. Hardware will keep predators away from the chickens and keep them safe. Adding hardware material of up to 3 feet is a good compromise if you can't afford to do so for the entire run. This will keep raccoons from squeezing in and stealing your chickens. The top of the run can be covered with chicken wire or strong twine in a random zigzag pattern if hawks or owls are an issue. It is inevitable that predators who dig their way in, such as foxes and coyotes, will try to dig their way out. It's better to dig a 6-inch trench around the run's perimeter to prevent this. Six inches of hardware cloth should be bent into an L-shape for each arm. Incorporating the wire into the ground once it's been attached to the foundation of the run area is discouraged.

Coop Security

It's essential that all doors to the coop have tamper-proof locks. You can keep predators out of your coop by locking the door and unlocking it with two opposing thumbs. Cover all vents with hardware material to keep out unwanted visitors. Periodically inspect the floors of your coops to make sure there are no holes that need to be repaired. In addition to eggs and chicks, rats and mice will gnaw their way into your coop to get to the food. Make sure to inspect the roof as well.

Ranging Your Hens

Raising chickens can be done in a variety of ways, from letting them roam free to keeping them fully cooped up. The best choice for you will be determined by where you live.

Free-Range

The term "free-range" refers to allowing your flock to forage freely on your property. There are no limits on how far they can go in any given location. Fences around your property may be the sole way to distinguish your land from your neighbors'.

Fenced Range

The term "fenced range" means that as long as the chickens stay inside the confines of a designated area, they are free to roam.

In addition to protecting the chickens from predators on the ground, the fence serves as a barrier.

Chicken Tractors

If you have a large yard and a small flock of hens, chicken tractors are a great option. A chicken tractor is a wheeled chicken coop. The ability to relocate makes life a little bit easier. After a few days of feeding the hens, you can move the chicken tractor to a new location. To help you get started, we've compiled a list of a few ideas.

Here are chicken tractor plans that anyone can build.

[27 DIY Chicken Tractor Plans](#)

[How to Build a Chicken Tractor](#)

[61 Free DIY Chicken Coop Plans & Ideas](#)

It's best to use a chicken tractor if you've got a lot of room. This will help the grass grow and eat away at bugs due to the aeration process. Another benefit is that you don't have to keep up with your chicken coop like you do with a stationary one.

Chicken Coops

First, determine the size of your coop and the surrounding area. Everything should be measured down to the smallest detail. Next, decide if you want to build or buy a coop.

Here are a few websites where you can purchase your ideal coop.

https://www.omlet.us/shop/chicken_keeping/portable-chicken-coop-eglu-go-up/

https://www.mypetchicken.com/catalog/Chicken-Coops-c3.aspx

Many other wooden coops are available. When purchasing chicken coops, you need to be careful. Do your research before making a purchase. Wooden coops are common but Plastic coop is easier for cleaning and maintenance, for example, it's harder to develop red mites in a plastic coop. Wooden coop has a traditional look and is cheaper than plastic. So both materials have pros and cons.

Creating Your Own Chicken Coop

Many people prefer to construct their own chicken coops because it gives them complete control of the final product. It's also possible to make your own chicken house out of separate sections. These are cost-effective and simple to maintain, and they make it harder for parasites to hide in wooden chicken coops, which are usually full of them. If you want to create your own chicken coop, you'll need a blueprint. DIY is a good way to keep prices down, especially if you're on a budget.

Construction supplies are needed to make chicken coops.

When selecting materials for your chicken coop, you should ask yourself the following questions:

-What's the price?

-Are the materials non-hazardous?

-Are they robust enough to withstand attacks from predators?

-Are they pest-resistant?

-Are they long-lasting?

Wood is commonly used in the construction of chicken coops. Compared with softwoods like pine and fir, hardwoods like redwood, cedar, and tropical wood are more resistant to pests. Most chicken coops are built from softwoods like pine. After that, non-toxic paint is used to coat the coop. Here are a few options for building a chicken coop from scratch.

https://www.thespruce.com/free-chicken-coop-plans-1357113

https://www.ecopeanut.com/diy-chicken-coop-plans/

https://backyardchickenproject.com/10-free-chicken-coop-plans/

A Backup Coop

In the event of an emergency, you should keep a smaller coop on hand. Things can come up unexpectedly, and you can use the backup chicken coop when they do. Backup coops are necessary for a variety of reasons:

-If a chicken is ill, it must be placed in isolation.

-A chicken may be a bully, so it must be isolated.

-If you have a rooster, you can utilize the second coop to give your hens a break in the second coop.

-If any of your chickens are injured, you can place them in the second coop.

-Your hen-hatching chicks can be placed in the second coop.

-You can place your chicks in the second coop until they are older.

-The second coop is necessary if you add one or two new chickens to your flock.   You can utilize the second coop to provide them with additional space.

Other Things to Keep in Mind

Feeders

It is best to use hanging feeders rather than feeders that are situated on the ground. Using this product will prevent mice and rats. For three chickens, you'll only need one feeder. Feeders should be set up for six chickens.

Waterers

Your chickens require a steady supply of water. Water is essential for chickens' health and egg production. Provide a plethora of waterers so that even the more submissive chickens can get their fill. Chickens can be kept warm by using heaters or waterers that have a heating system built into them if you live in a chilly climate.

Toys

Behavioral issues can arise if chickens are bored. Give your hens a chance to practice their agility. To keep your hens entertained, consider enrolling them in one of these classes. Getting to know your chickens in this way is also a fun way to spend time with them.

https://www.youtube.com/watch?v=ReC85qqSpHA

https://www.youtube.com/watch?v=cUc2N6drj2E

To keep your chickens from getting bored, provide them with a variety of scratching posts. Keep them occupied with mounds of straw or leaves during the autumn.

Dust Bath

Chickens require regular dust baths. For them, it's a big deal. They use it as a means of removing parasites from their bodies. A good dust wash is essential for chickens, or they will become stressed. A few chickens can be comfortably bathed in a dust bath that is no more than 1 or 2 inches deep. Chickens' favorite toys are dust baths in the form of bowls. Both inside and outside the coop are viable options. Using a boot tray or an under-the-sink mat for an inside dust bath is a brilliant idea:

Certain folks may find it common practice to dig a hole in the coop and fill it with sand. For dust baths, use materials like baking soda and vinegar. Here are some other options for dust bath materials:

Fine dirt/ Wood ash/ Diatomaceous earth/ Dried lemon balm or dried lavender

Egg Crates

If you're keeping eggs, you'll need egg crates. For small flocks, a single basket suffices, but for bigger ones, egg crates are required.

Bedding

Your chickens will lay more eggs if they are more comfortable, which can be achieved by providing them with bedding. Cedar shavings should not be used because they are poisonous to chickens.

What is the purpose of bedding?

Catching the poop/ Insulation/ Encourages egg production in your chickens in the nest boxes/ With bedding, chickens can stay inside of the coop if they don't want to go outside.

Bedding needs to be:

Relatively inexpensive/ Quick-drying/ Non-toxic/ Absorbent/ Compostable

Wood Shavings

A feed shop or a local woodworker can provide you with wood shavings. Chickens enjoy scratching around in wood shavings because it makes them feel at ease. Additionally, wood shavings remain dry and odorless, even when chicken feces are around. However, sawdust should not be used. It generates a great deal of dust, which causes respiratory issues in the hens.

Hay or Straw

You can give your chickens straw or hay to sleep on as a bedding material. Hay is expensive because it is the principal food source for cows. Straw is readily available. It's a bargain or even free. To save money, you can use straws as a bed for your pets. For the chickens, nothing beats a nice, cozy blanket of straw. Make sure there are no pests or insects in the straw you choose.

Sand

Sand is a popular choice for some people regarding chicken bedding. However, it is not ideal. When it gets wet, it becomes too heavy to absorb chicken dung. As a result, the chickens have difficulty. Do not play in the sand for sandboxes.

Diatomaceous Earth (DE)

Chicken coops are commonly disinfected with diatomaceous earth (DE). It's possible to find natural DE at the bottom of the seabed. Industrial-grade DE is also available for cleaning and industrial purposes. Your hens may have issues if you put commercial DE on them. Make sure the diatomaceous earth you purchase is food-grade.

Things to consider when using DE:

-Do not use it excessively. Avoid overcrowding your coop with DE.

-Ensure that your coop has adequate airflow.

-Apply DE to the dust bath outside the chicken coop if you have multiple dust baths.

-The DE should be sprinkled rather than poured.

-Before spraying DE, chickens must be removed from the coop.

Tips for using DE:

-Use a small amount of DE rather than a large amount all at once.

-Keep the DE dry.

-Do not use DE if you have a deep litter system.

Materials to Avoid

Cider shavings: The natural cedar oil found in cedar shavings is toxic to hens.

Sawdust: Sawdust is great for composting but not for use as bedding. The health of your poultry is jeopardized by sawdust.

4

Choosing Your Chicken Breeds

In this chapter, we'll cover the best chicken breeds for beginners. Your first flock of chickens will be incomplete without the proper selection of birds.

There are mainly three types of chickens available:

Laying hens: These are raised for eggs.

Fryers: These are raised for meat.

Dual: These are used to produce both eggs and meat. They usually lay eggs for a couple of years; then, you can use them as meat hens.

If you're going to keep a rooster, you'll need to decide. Roosters are not allowed in many towns. Find out what the rules are. Once the rooster has been introduced, you're done.

Australorp

Dual: Australorps are dual-purpose chickens.

Features: Chicken farmers like them because of their temperaments and egg production. As a beginner chicken farmer, Australorps is an excellent choice for you. You will need more space for your chickens.

Size: Large

Eggs: 5 to 6 eggs every week

Egg color: Brown

Coping ability with humans: Tame, kid-friendly

Coping ability with the flock: Calm and not aggressive

Climate tolerance: Cold hardy

Availability and cost: Common

Rhode Island Red

Dual: Similar to Australorps, this breed also has a dual purpose.

Features: They can get agitated sometimes.

Size: Medium

Eggs: 5 large eggs per week

Egg color: Brown

Coping ability with humans: Friendly, kid-friendly

Coping ability with the flock: Bossy, likes to dominate

Climate tolerance: Can tolerate any type of climate

Availability and cost: Common

Plymouth Rock

Dual: Another dual-purpose chicken

Features: This is a good choice for beginner chicken farmers. They are very cooperative and not prone to being broody (not prone to wanting their eggs to hatch).

Size: Large

Eggs: 4 eggs per week

Egg color: Light brown

Coping ability with humans: Friendly, tame

Coping ability with the flock: Not aggressive

Climate tolerance: Cold tolerant

Availability and cost: Common

Speckled Sussex

Dual: Originated in Sussex, England, it is a dual-purpose chicken.

Features: Broodiness is a problem for these hens. They are very curious and can get bored if you do not offer them entertainment.

Size: Large

Eggs: 4 eggs per week

Egg color: Light brown

Coping ability with humans: Gentle, kid-friendly

Coping ability with the flock: Friendly

Climate tolerance: Can tolerate both types of climates

Availability and cost: Common

Wyandottes

This is another breed that is popular with chicken farmers.

Dual: These chickens are medium build but stocky, so you will get a lot of meat.

Features: They are a really good choice as an egg-producing and meat-producing chicken. The Wyandotte is quieter, and if you have only a small space in an urban setting, then choose this variety.

Size: Large and heavy

Eggs: 4 medium-sized eggs per week

Egg color: Cream color

Coping ability with humans: Chicken farmers often describe these chickens as "aloof." They do not show aggressive behavior.

Coping ability with the flock: They try to be dominant but not aggressive with other chickens. They are not bullies but will react when provoked. You need to choose calmer chickens if you want to raise them in your flock.

Climate tolerance: Can tolerate all types of climates.

Availability and cost: Common

Leghorns

Layer

Features: This breed is used to produce eggs. If you have a smaller area to raise your chickens, then a few of them will give you enough eggs for a small family.

Size: Medium

Eggs: 4 eggs per week

Egg color: White

Coping ability with humans: This breed is very independent. If you want to cuddle your chickens, then they are not for you.

Coping ability with the flock: They are not aggressive.

Climate tolerance: They can tolerate heat but can't tolerate cold climates.

Availability and cost: Common

Dominique/Pilgrim Fowl

Dual: This is one of the oldest breeds in the US.

Features: Broody

Size: Medium

Eggs: 4 medium-sized eggs per week

Egg color: Brown

Coping ability with humans: They are very calm. They can mix with children easily, so they are a good choice for a family.

Coping ability with the flock: Not aggressive

Climate tolerance: Very cold, hardy

Availability and cost: Very common

Buff Orpington

Dual

Features: Great mothers. Their calm nature makes them vulnerable to overeating and weight gain. Do not give them too much food.

Size: Large

Eggs: 3 to 4 large eggs per week

Egg color: Brown

Coping ability with humans: Tame and affectionate. Kid-friendly.

Coping ability with the flock: They are very calm, so be careful when mixing them with aggressive hens. Do not mix them with dominant breeds such as Welsummers or Rhode Island Reds.

Climate tolerance: Very cold, hardy

Availability and cost: Common

Jersey Giant

Fryer

Features: Broody. They are good parents.

Size: This is the largest chicken

Eggs: Around 4 large eggs per week

Egg color: Light/medium brown

Coping ability with humans: Friendly. This bird is very gentle. They are so big that it makes it hard for a child to carry them.

Coping ability with the flock: They are not aggressive. Their size ensures that they will not end up at the bottom of the hierarchy.

Climate tolerance: Very cold, hardy but can't tolerate too much heat.

Availability and cost: Common

Isa Browns

Layer: This type of breed is used to produce eggs.

Features: They produce a lot of eggs. Isa Browns are friendly towards humans but do not like motherhood. You need to use an incubator to hatch chicks.

Size: Medium

Eggs: 4 to 5 eggs per week

Egg color: Brown

Coping ability with humans: Kid-friendly. Affectionate with humans.

Coping ability with the flock: They behave well with their own breed. But they can be aggressive with other breeds of chickens. If you want a breed that produces a lot of eggs, then this is the chicken for you.

Climate tolerance: Winter hardy. They can tolerate hot weather if you provide them with plenty of water and shade.

Availability and cost: Common

Welsummers

Chicken farmers like to raise them for their egg production, but they are not for beginners.

Dual

Features: They are quiet so you can raise them in the suburbs.

Size: Medium

Eggs: 4 eggs per week

Egg color: Dark brown

Coping ability with humans: They are not unfriendly but also not tame. They are not kid-friendly.

Coping ability with the flock: They can become bullies to other breeds.

Climate Tolerance: Cold hardy

Availability and cost: Not very expensive. You can collect them online.

Salmon Faverolles

Fryer: They are meat hens

Features: They are vocal. They can go broody.

Size: Large

Eggs: 4 eggs per week

Egg color: Light brown

Coping ability with humans: Kid-friendly. They like to cuddle. They are very gentle and playful.

Coping ability with the flock: Do not raise them in a mixed-breed environment because they will be at the bottom of the hierarchy.

Climate Tolerance: Cold hardy

Availability and cost: This breed is popular.

Easter Eggers

They are a hybrid of breeds.

Layer

Features: The noise that they make depends on the type of chicken you have. They are curious, and you need to supply them with toys to keep them interested.

Size: Small

Eggs: 4 to 5 eggs per week

Egg color: It depends on the hybrid you have. Colors can be lavender, purple, pink, olive green, aqua, blue, etc.

Coping ability with humans: Kid-friendly and friendly towards humans. They can be fun chickens to raise.

Coping ability with the flock: They are gentle and not bullies. If you want to raise them with other breeds, then choose calm breeds like Cochins or Faverolles.

Climate tolerance: Can tolerate both heat and cold

Availability and cost: Common

Cochin

Fryer

Features: They do not like mud. They love motherhood. They will even happily hatch the eggs of other breeds. They can become broody when they are not busy hatching eggs.

Size: Large

Eggs: 2 medium- to large-sized eggs per week

Egg color: Brown

Coping ability with humans: Kid-friendly and very gentle. Too big for young children.

Coping ability with the flock: They are not bullies. Their size ensures that they do not end up at the bottom of the hierarchy.

Climate tolerance: Not especially heat tolerant but cold hardy. You need to provide plenty of water and shade during hot weather.

Availability and cost: Common

Brahmas

Dual

Features: They tend to the chicks and are broody. They are docile and cooperative.

Size: Very large, close to Jersey Giants

Eggs: 3 to 4 eggs per week

Egg color: Brown

Coping ability with humans: Kid-friendly. Very calm and gentle.

Coping ability with the flock: They have a calming influence in the flock.

Climate tolerance: Suitable for both hot and cold weather. However, they can't tolerate wet or muddy conditions because of their feathered legs. You need to provide them with care in the winter.

Availability and cost: Easy to find

Polish

Neither fryer nor layer nor dual

Features: They are a lot of fun. Kids love them because of their cooperative nature.

Size: Small

Eggs: 2 to 3 medium-sized eggs per week on average. It depends on the chicken.

Egg color: White

Coping ability with humans: Kid-friendly. Great as a pet.

Coping ability with the flock: They will end up at the bottom of the hierarchy because of their small size. Do not mix them with aggressive or dominant chickens.

Climate tolerance: Not cold hardy. Their crown gets wet in the winter and freezes.

Availability and cost: Easy to get

Bantam Breeds

Most breeds have a smaller size Bantam variety.

Fryer

Features: The Silkie Bantam chicken is adorable. They cannot fly and will get broody.

Size: Small

Eggs: 3 medium-sized eggs per week

Egg color: White/cream

Coping ability with humans: Very kid-friendly and wonderful pets

Coping ability with the flock: Because of their gentle nature and small stature, they often end up on the low end of the hierarchy. Do not put them with dominant breeds.

Climate tolerance: Both heat and cold hardy. However, they are not water tolerant. Always keep them dry.

Availability and cost: You can find them regionally.

Frizzles

Not all frizzle chickens look similar to the above chicken. Others have different colors or crowns.

Looker: Show chicken

Features: They are adorable and comical. They can't fly

Size: Small or medium

Eggs: 2 to 3 medium-sized eggs per week

Egg color: Cream

Coping ability with humans: Kid-friendly and gentle. Raisers often describe them as sweet.

Coping ability with the flock: You can mix them with other chickens like them, such as Polish, Silkies, and Cochins.

Climate tolerance: They can't tolerate extreme heat or cold. They like moderate temperatures.

Availability and cost: Available

Buying from Online Hatcheries

You should be cautious when purchasing from online hatcheries. The first step is to find a trustworthy hatchery. Keep in mind that hatcheries are in the business of mass-producing chickens. Keep your dog with a reputable breeder, as many breeders aren't concerned about upholding the breed standard. Learn about backyard chickens by checking out online forums.

I would love to hear from you!

It's through your support and reviews that my book is able to reach the haands of other readres too. Please take 60 seconds to kindly leave a review on Amazon. Please scan the QR code below. If you reside in a country that isn't listed, please use the link provided in your Amazon order.

Please follow these simple steps to rate/review my book:

1. Open your camera on your phone
2. Hover it over the QR code below
3. Rate/review my book

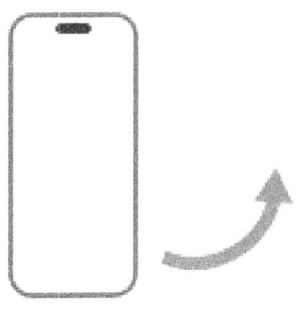

All it takes is 60 seconds to make a difference!

5

BRINGING YOUR CHICKS HOME

When you bring your chicks home for the first time, the first question you should ask is: How long until they lay their first egg? Here are some guidelines for getting started with chicken care.

Basic Chicken Needs

Before the arrival of your chicks, you must prepare a brooder box for them. This can be a customized cardboard box, a plastic tote, or another comparable container. They must be safe from predators (including domesticated animals), preferably in a somewhat quiet, secure environment. If you have a secure garage or shady area, that will suffice. Some individuals put the incubator in a spare room or basement.

You will need to provide the chicks with bedding. It may consist of wood shavings, newspaper shreds, finely chopped straws, or peat moss. The bedding should be odorless, absorbent, and reasonably priced. The number of feeders and waterers required for the chicks will depend on how many chicks you acquire. A round screw-on feeder can feed up to eight chicks with ease, and the same can be said for the drinker. Finally, you will require a heat source. This could be either a broiler plate or a heat lamp. The plate for the brooder is more expensive, but it is safer.

Bringing Home Chicks

If you ordered your chicks by mail, you should be told when they were shipped and when to anticipate their arrival. You must use the heat source for many hours prior to the arrival of the chicks to ensure that the temperature is optimal. If you are transporting them from the store to your home, put on the heat immediately and monitor them constantly for the first several hours. If your chicks are huddled beneath the bulb, the temperature is too low. If they have spread out to the boundaries of the incubator, the temperature is too high.

Adjust the temperature until the chicks are dispersed throughout the incubator. A thermometer should read between 90 and 95°F. Continue to drop the temperature by 5 to 10 degrees per week until the 6th week, when it should be around 65°F. When placing the chicks in their new home for the first time, quickly submerge their beaks in the water so they know where it is. They will not drink hot water, so do not place the water beneath the heat lamp. You will need to direct them to the meal. This can be accomplished by sprinkling crumbs near the food dispenser.

Managing your Chickens

In the coming weeks, it is crucial that you understand how and when to handle your chicks. This is a key step in the process of bonding and will help you develop your lifelong relationship with them.

Children and Chicks

Children's desire to pet chicks. However, ensure that they do it carefully, as the respiratory system of a bird differs greatly from that of a human. If the chicks are held or compressed too firmly, they can quickly suffocate. Additionally, children should not chase or torment chicks.

Learning about You

You must familiarize yourself with the ladies. Start by placing some food in the palm of your hand on the floor of the incubator. As long as you maintain your position, they will investigate. After a couple of days, they should not be terrified of your hand, so try softly petting them as they sit or stand on your hand. By the end of the week, chicks should identify your hands with positive experiences and feel at ease around them. Continue making gradual progress by momentarily taking them up and rewarding them when you set them down. You can extend the duration of their daily hold. Eventually, they will approach you for collection and a reward.

From the Incubator to the Coop

At roughly 6 to 8 weeks, they should have their first complete set of feathers and be able to regulate their own body temperature. This is the optimal moment to transfer them from the brooder to the chicken coop. If you intend to house them with larger birds, they must be at least two-thirds the size of the adults, roughly as same size as the smallest one of your flock.

Make sure that older hens don't transmit disease to chicks. New chicks and the existing flocks should be kept separate for about 30 days. Chicks might take for 18 weeks to grow bigger.

Chicks must be able to flee from larger birds that would likely attempt to peck or torment them. One approach to assisting them is to provide ample escape space and higher perches from which they can fly to safety. Set up a safe, fenced space where the chicks may become accustomed to the outside sounds and sights prior to integrating them into an existing flock. Also, place the two groups in side-by-side runs. Placing the two groups next to one another for one week can help the birds form bonds before being housed together. The chickens can be kept outside during the day and placed in the brooder at night.

When they are ready to move outside permanently, keep them inside their coop for the first 24 hours. The rationale for this is that spending 24 hours in their coop will make them realize that it is their home. In the end, they will happily return to the coop every night when you let them out of their pen. Before shutting the chickens in the coop for 24 hours, ensure that there is food and water available.

Exploring their Surroundings

Naturally, chicks are curious but wary. Due to their lack of experience with the world's perils, chicks are not as careful as adults. Once chicks are large enough to leave the brooder box and enter their own coop, it is your responsibility to ensure their safety. It must be predator-proof and contain everything necessary for the chicks' survival. Ensure there are no tight spots where a chick could become trapped. They will explore their new habitat slowly at first, but by the second day, they should feel at ease. Create perches and roosting bars at chick height initially, then elevate them as necessary. If you intend to let your chickens roam freely, it is best that they recognize the coop as their home. Therefore, restrict them for around 1 week until they become accustomed to the routine.

Providing Them with a Pen

Permit your chicks to spend 24 hours in their coop. Then, acquaint them with their run/pen. This will allow you to become more acquainted with your chicks. Do not forcibly remove your chickens from the coop. Simply unlock the door and wait. Keep food and water in their enclosure to encourage them to go outside.

The curious chicks will be the first to escape the coop and investigate. The remaining sheep will join them later. However, if the flock does not leave after a few hours, then gently force them outside.

Once darkness falls, you must return your chicks to their coop. Typically, when night falls, the chicks return to their coop on their own. If your chicks are not yet in their coop, gently coax them inside by pushing on them. Reintroduce your chicks to their coop in a calm and careful manner. For the next week, you must coax your chicks out of the coop in the morning and back in before dusk.

Your chicks will settle in beautifully after 1 week. If you want your chicks to roam freely, remove the pen and allow them to do so. Every day, ensure that your chicks leave the coop in the morning and return before dusk.

For the first few days, create a little area where they can walk around and become acquainted with the outside. If your chicks do not return on their own, tempt them into the coop with their preferred food, such as mealworms. It is best for the chicks to be free-range, but they must be vigilant for hawks and other predators. The best answer overall is to leave them in a covered run when you cannot supervise them.

6

Providing Nutrition and Water

Feeding Poultry: A Comprehensive Guide

What Do Chickens Eat?

Just like us, chickens can be described as omnivores. Consequently, it stands to reason that they would eat a wide variety of plant and animal matter, including seeds, insects, earthworms, snails, and even a few species of frog and mouse.

Grit

Insoluble grit is important in the gizzard of chickens, even though it has little nutritional value. Because chickens lack teeth, they are unable to grind their food properly on their own and require assistance. Grit is ingested spontaneously by wild chickens when they peck at insects, worms, and other such organisms. Food is ground into mush by the grit in the gizzard, which acts like teeth. Muscle makes up a gizzard pouch. It's in the gizzard that the food grinds against the chips of stone as the muscle pushes it. In a way, it's like a mill's grinding wheel.

Chicks

Commercial starter feed usually eliminates the requirement for grit in broiler chicks. Without grinding, the feed for chickens is already small enough to be easily digested. Grit will be required when chicks grow and are fed kitchen scraps or mealworm snacks. Chickens should not be fed anything other than commercial feed until they are at least 3 to 4 months old, as this can lead to an imbalance in their diet. For chicks under 3 weeks old, you can use washed construction sand as grit. A crop's growth can be harmed if the sand used in play areas is too fine. Chick grit that is coarser than what they need as adults can be purchased 3 weeks after hatching. It's fine to feed the baby chick grit for the first 2 months. After that, it's time to offer the kids some adult grit.

Adult Chickens

Even if you solely feed your chickens commercial chicken feed, you should still give them grit. Make sure you obtain the correct grade of grit from your feed store if you're feeding an adult bird. The meal will not be broken down if the grit is too fine and will just pass through the grinder. Birds living in the wild may not need grit, because they have access to stones in their surroundings. Grit for your chickens, on the other hand, is a good supplement because you don't know how much they're getting.

How to Give Grit a Good Start

Add some grit to their meals. Make sure it's clean, and restock it as needed.

Oyster Shell

Calcium is needed to develop strong bones and hard eggshells. Feeding ground oyster shells to your chickens is one of the simplest methods to ensure that they are getting the calcium they need. Chickens that are soon to be producing eggs do not need oyster shells. Grit, on the other hand, does not dissolve in the intestines. It is possible for an eggshell to be too soft if a hen does not get enough calcium, which can induce egg binding. Even though commercial meals contain calcium, they are not sufficient for egg production. Oyster shells can be pounded into a fine powder and served to your chickens in a bowl, just like grit.

Essential Nutrition

Chicken feed, like a human diet, needs to be diverse and balanced to be healthy. Commercial chicken feed is the only diet for many chickens, who consume it for the duration of their lives. Commercial chicken feed is a complete diet carefully adjusted by poultry nutritionists in order to provide your chickens with all of the vital nutrients they require. There are different kinds of feed made for animals at different ages and stages of development.

Chickens necessitate six nutrients in their diet:

Protein/ Carbohydrates/ Fat/ Vitamins/ Minerals/ Water

Chickens, like other animals, need to eat to keep their bodies strong and healthy as they grow and mature. They wouldn't be able to do anything if they didn't have power. Every single one of their activities necessitates the consumption of nutrients. In addition, energy is required for the formation of skin, bone, feathers, and eggs. There is no way they could survive without proper nutrition. Because protein, carbohydrates, and fat contain carbon, hydrogen, and oxygen, they can all be used as energy sources. You'll get roughly 4 kcal of energy per gram of protein or carbs you consume. Fat can supply up to 9 kcal per gram more, which is why high-quality fat sources are required in feed formulations. Better outcomes can be achieved with less feed when it is made from high-quality, nutrient-dense ingredients. Let's take a closer look at the six most important food groups in a chicken's diet.

Protein

Amino acids are the small, complicated molecules that make up protein. When the bird eats, its digestive tract breaks its food down into amino acids, which are taken into the bloodstream and carried to cells throughout the body. Chickens need particular proteins to build muscle, skin, feathers, cartilage, and even egg whites. In order for your backyard flock to grow properly, they need all of the essential amino acids, with lysine and methionine being the most crucial. In commercial feed, the most frequent sources of protein include corn gluten, canola soybeans, field pea meal, flax, lupins, sunflower seeds, and insects.

Carbohydrates

Carbohydrates are the chicken's most convenient source of energy. Cells in the body favor them as a source of power. Poultry feed is primarily composed of carbohydrates. Cereals like sorghum, millet, wheat, corn, barley, and rye are used to make them. Starch and sugar are examples of digestible carbs, andcellulose is an example of an indigestible carb.

Fat

In terms of caloric content, fat is the most abundant. Saturated and unsaturated fats are both forms of fat. Poultry feed is the primary source of saturated fat, which is solid at room temperature. Unsaturated fats are liquids, in contrast to saturated fats, which are solids. Veggie oils and nuts are the sources of these fatty acids. Fat is necessary for the absorption of vitamins that are only fat-soluble. Fat also aids in the reduction of grain dust and improves the palatability of the feed.

Vitamins

Vitamins are minimally required by chickens. In food, you'll find organic molecules like these that are necessary for a healthy body and proper growth and reproduction. Many health issues might arise as a result of vitamin deficiency. Vitamins A, D, E, and K are fat-soluble vitamins, and vitamins C and all of the B vitamins are water-soluble. Vitamin C, for example, can be synthesized within the bird. Some vitamins, such as vitamin D, can be made by the body when exposed to sunshine, but others must be obtained through food.

Minerals

Minerals, like vitamins, are only needed in trace amounts. They aid in the flow of blood, metabolism, and the functioning of muscles. There are two types of minerals: macrominerals and microminerals. Egg-laying hens need calcium to produce eggs with a hard shell. It is common for grains to be added to commercial feeds due to their lack of mineral content. As an extra source of calcium, layer birds should also be given powdered oyster shells.

Water

Your chickens need clean, fresh water at all times. Water makes up the majority of the blood's composition. It carries important nutrients from the digestive tract to the organs and tissues. Lack of water can reduce egg production and harm your bird's health, even for a short time. Chicken nipples are the best and simplest way to supply clean water to your flock. Unlike other watering devices, chicken nipple waterers keep the water clear of debris and algae. Additionally, their design prevents disease transmission, which is common in open waterers. If you live in a region in which winter temperatures drop below freezing, chicken nipple waterers are an excellent choice. It is advisable to use chicken nipples as a waterer for chickens.

Different Types of Chicken Feed

The best way to feed chickens a balanced and nutritious diet is to purchase a commercial feed formulated specifically for the breed of chicken you have. Even though it may be tempting to prepare your own homemade chicken feed, it can be difficult and expensive to meet all of your chickens' nutritional requirements. Feeds like Mile Four Feeds meet all of your flock's nutritional requirements. The dietary needs of a chicken fluctuate with age, season, and general health. It is not necessary to supplement commercial feed with anything other than an oyster shell for laying hens, but it is still recommended to use grit to help digestion. To keep things interesting and prevent boredom, consider giving out some sweets. Every stage of a chicken's life is catered to by a commercial chicken feed. Using a different brand may yield somewhat different results. Among the most common are:

Chick Starter

Chick starter feed is given to chicks from the time they hatch until they reach the next stage of their lives, such as laying eggs. For chickens that will lay eggs, chick beginning feeds typically contain about 20% protein. There is a broiler starter available for meat birds that has a protein value of 22% to 24%. You can buy medicated or unmedicated chicken starters.

Medicated Feed

Chick starter meals that contain preventative agents against coccidiosis are supposed to assist chicks in developing immunity to the disease. Adult chickens who have been exposed to coccidiosis and are now immune to the parasite (protozoa) can transmit coccidiosis through their feces. Coccidiosis is a parasitic disease that can be lethal to hens because it destroys the gut wall. Feeding with the anti-coccidia drug amprolium is used to stop the spread of coccidia in the chick's digestive system.

Chick starter feed may be beneficial for my chickens, but is it necessary?

Soil-borne coccidiosis can arise in naturally occurring populations. You should use a medicated starter feed if you have ever had a proven case of coccidiosis in your flock. If you're not sure if the soil you're planting in has coccidiosis, you can also use medicated starter feed. Feeding medicinal feed to chicks in a brooder, where they are not exposed to dirt or other chickens, is unsuccessful.

Coccidiosis or contaminated dirt must be present for the medication to work. You can feed the chicks unmedicated chick starters while they're in the brooder. In order to avoid coccidiosis, you should give your chicks a medicated chick starter a few weeks before you take them outside or add dirt to their brooder. Until your chickens have graduated to a grower or layer meal, provide medicated chick starter feed.

Layer Grower

A layer or starter feed can be introduced to your newborn chickens when they are 6 weeks old. Future laying hens will grow slowly so that their bones and internal organs can develop properly. Too much protein in a feed might lead to premature laying in chickens. Don't worry if you can't find a pullet grower's feed. In most cases, chick starter diets are fed to birds until they are at least 6 months old or have begun to lay eggs. Chick starter can be used as a substitute for pullet growers if it is not available in your area. Most of the time, meat birds like Cornish hens and broilers are fed a diet that has 18% protein.

Layer Developer/Finisher

Before they begin laying at 14 weeks, layer pullets can be fed a 16% protein layer diet. Some feed companies don't separate their grower and finisher feeds and instead blend them into one.

Layer Feed

Breeds of laying hens typically reach sexual maturity between 20 and 22 weeks of age. When they're this young, they need a protein-rich diet with additional calcium and minerals. Shell-strong eggs can be produced by feeding layer feed. To avoid kidney injury, wait until your chicks are about 20 weeks old or when they begin laying eggs before switching them to a layer diet. Layer feed can also be given to roosters.

Broiler Feed

Meat birds require a considerably higher protein diet than layer birds because they grow quickly and require a lot of calories. For broiler growers and finishers, the feed typically contains between 18 and 20% protein. After 12 weeks of age, heritage or free-range birds can be fed a lower protein diet of 16%.

Feather Fixer Feed

When birds go through a molt in the fall, Feather Fixer feed is designed to provide them with the nutrition they need. It helps feathers grow tough and eggshells stay hard. Feeding it at any time of year is possible as well.

Flock Feed: Feeding of the Entire Flock

Chickens, ducks, and turkeys are all part of a mixed flock, and all flock feed is designed to meet the needs of these birds. It can also be used as a turkey finisher because of its high protein content, which typically ranges between 17% and 18%.

Chickens can be fed pellets.

Scratch Grain

Rather than being used as a primary dietary source, scratch grain is meant to be a treat. Foraging for food is an essential part of hens' natural behavior. Scratch grain—a mixture of grains and seeds such as broken corn, wheat, barley, or oats—is used to encourage this habit. Scratch grain may be compared to candy or quick food for hens because of its low-protein, high-energy content. Too much scratch grain can break the delicate balance in commercial feeds, which are precisely prepared. It's best to stick to the 90:10 rule: 90% commercial feed, 10% scratch grain at all times. Grit, which is important for digestion, must also be added to scratch grain.

Pellets vs. Crumbles vs. Mash

The terms "pellets," "crumbles," and "mash" all relate to the amount of food that is being fed. The largest in size, pellets, are cylinder-shaped pellets. Smaller, fragmented, pellet-like fragments are known as "crumbles." Chicken feed in the form of mash is the smallest and most loosely ground. There is no difference in the nutritional value of pellets, crumbles, or mash. For example, an apple can be eaten whole (pellets), chopped up into pieces (crumbles), or minced up (mash). A common practice is to feed chicks and young birds mash and crumbles because they are easier to eat. Mash, crumbles, or pellets can be used to feed birds that are older than 6 months. There is another type of chicken feed that isn't often used: whole grain. Cracked grain and unprocessed components are used to make whole grain feed. Whole grain feed is different from pellets, crumbles, and mash in that you can clearly see all of the ingredients.

Specialty Feeds

There are a variety of specialty chicken diets available, including organic, soy-free, corn-free, and non-GMO options. Commercial chicken feed typically costs less than this form of feed. Pesticides are not used in organic chicken feed. Organic chicken feed is manufactured from grains that haven't been sprayed with chemicals, just like organic food at the grocery store. Soy- and corn-free meals can help chicken owners who are allergic or sensitive to soy or maize. Some people are sensitive to store-bought eggs because they are fed a diet of maize and soy. These people may be able to consume eggs if the chickens are fed a diet free of soy and/or corn. There are no genetically modified grains in non-GMO chicken feed.

Fermented Chicken Feed

Some of you may be familiar with the concept of fermenting chicken feed. Fermented chicken feed is an at-home approach for making healthier and longer-lasting chicken feed. It is not a commercially available product. Feed for chickens that has been steeped in water for 2 or 3 days is known as fermented chicken feed. Adding probiotics and making the meal more digestible are both achieved through the soaking procedure. You may save money and enhance the health of your chickens by fermenting all sorts of chicken feed.

Treats for Chickens

Despite the fact that chicken feed contains all of the necessary nutrients, many people prefer to give their chickens treats instead. Some of the most common threats are:

Kitchen scraps/ Scratch grain/ Grubbies/ Mealworms/ Sunflower seeds

Kitchen Scraps

Although many backyard chickens are fed kitchen waste, this practice is fine if you're careful. Even though they're supposed to be safe, some chicken treats can be deadly. There is a danger in eating a large portion of avocado, especially the pit and peel. Foods such as chocolate, raw or undercooked vegetables (especially green potatoes and their skins/peelings), fruits and vegetable bars, dried or uncooked legumes (save for thoroughly cooked baked beans), moldy or rotting food, and highly processed food and meat must also be avoided. If you feed your chickens a lot of table scraps, such as lettuce or bread, they may not be able to produce as many eggs. Chickens should only be fed 15 to 20 minutes' worth of kitchen scraps at a time. Botulism can be dangerous if a chicken eats rotten or moldy scraps. Chickens enjoy "candy" in the form of scratch grains, which should be provided in moderation.

How Much to Feed Your Chickens

Your chickens' age and the quality of the feed you offer will determine how much food they need. In general, six adult chickens require roughly 1.5 pounds of food each day, or about 1/4 pound of food for each bird.

How to Feed Chickens

A treadle feeder is the most convenient tool for feeding hens. Using a step-activated door, a treadle feeder lets chickens get to the food within. Because they shield the food from rain and snow and keep rodents and wild birds out, treadle feeders are the best choice for hens. Chickens can consume as much food as they like because their feeders are large enough to hold a lot of food. Feeding chicks in a dish or feeder is preferable to sprinkling food bits on the ground. Diseases can spread more easily when hens are fed from the ground because the feed is likely to be contaminated with feces. The feed should be level with the chickens' backs when hanging a feeder from a tree branch or other sturdy object.

Aside from preventing bird damage, this should keep rats out of your bird food as well. Chickens that are shyer may not acquire enough food if the feeders are placed in a limited area or against a wall. It's best not to store your feed in the coop itself. Place it in the coop or a place where the chickens have access to the outside. The purpose of this is to keep rats out of the henhouse. Chickens don't eat in the evenings, which is an excellent time for rats to feast, so it's better to remove the food at night. The disease can be spread to your flock by wild birds. Keeping them out of your chicken coop and away from the feed is the best course of action in this situation. In order to feed chickens, they should be fed from a dish or feed container. Avoid having them scavenge on the ground for food.

Storing Chicken Feed

Store chicken feed in a dry location and in a sealed container to avoid rodent or insect contamination. Many feed bags aren't waterproof against weather, so they shouldn't be left out. Chickens should never be fed rotten feed. A metal garbage can is the most convenient container for storing poultry feed. Rodents can't gnaw through metal trash cans because they're weather-resistant. Feed cans can hold up to three 40-pound or two 50-pound bags.

7

LAYING HEN MANAGEMENT

The Procedure of Raising Hens for Egg Production

Raising hens for egg production necessitates familiarizing yourself with the flock's production capacity. Determine how many eggs you may expect to produce by taking into account the various factors that affect egg production. A good hen-keeper should know which hens are laying and why other hens aren't and how to fix it. You can help your flock succeed if you have a clear knowledge of these variables.

Production Variables and Expectations that Have an Impact on Production

A hen can only produce one egg per day, and there will be some days when she will not lay any eggs at all. The hen's reproductive mechanism is the cause of this laying schedule. Approximately 26 hours after the previous egg is laid, a hen's body begins developing an egg. Because of this, hens will typically start laying their eggs later and later each day. Because the hen's reproductive system is light-sensitive, she will eventually start laying eggs too late at night, which will prevent her body from commencing the development of an egg. The hen will not lay for some days after that.

A flock's hens don't all start laying at the same time, and they don't all lay for the same period of time. The flock begins to produce swiftly, reaches a peak, and then gradually decreases its output. How many eggs a flock can produce and how long the flock lasts are both dependent on a variety of factors, including:

Breed/ Management of pullets before laying/ Light management/ Nutrition/ Space allowances

Breed

An egg-producing chicken breed is commercially viable. These birds are used in large egg production facilities, but backyard flocks often struggle with White Leghorns. To put it mildly, they're just too quick and prone to chaotic behavior. Eggs with white shells are also produced by these birds. It's not uncommon for consumers who buy eggs from small flocks to opt for brown eggs despite the fact that there are no nutritional differences between brown and white eggs. Commercial brown-shelled egg layers have been produced by breeders, some of which have been specifically bred for pastured poultry production.

Many hatcheries also sell sex-link crosses as a common product. Crosses allow the hatchery to classify chicks depending on feather color even before they've hatched. As a result, fewer sexing mistakes are made, lowering the likelihood that you'll end up with an unwanted hen. Some people choose to keep a mixed flock of birds. The eggs of these birds come in a wide range of colors. Eggs laid by Plymouth Rocks and Rhode Island Reds, two breeds commonly used for both brooding and laying, have light brown shells. In recent years, dark chocolate–colored egg shells laid by Maran hens have gained popularity. The Araucana is a South American bird with no tail and tufts of feathers on its head that lays pale blue eggs.

Using Araucanas and other breeds, "Easter Eggers" have been made that produce eggs with shells that are either light blue, green, or pink. As a result of these crossbreeds, these chickens have beards and muffs instead of the tufts found in Araucanas. An Ameraucana whose eggs are blue-green in color is the result of purebred crosses like these. If you're looking to raise chickens, keep in mind that although commercial breeds may provide you with a higher initial yield, alternative varieties tend to lay for a longer length of time.

Pullet Management

Pullet care, particularly in the areas of nutrition and light management, can have a significant impact on the quality and amount of eggs hens produce. A flock's overall health may suffer if young chicks are introduced to production too soon and develop prolapse problems. The hens may also produce a reduced number of eggs during the manufacturing process. A day-old chick is capable of maturing into an adult bird. For future laying flocks, proper light management must be implemented from hatching through all of the laying periods. It is imperative that you learn about the nutrition and light management of the pullets you are purchasing so that you may adjust the management of your flock properly. The use of light stimulation can be delayed if the chicks are too young.

Light Management to Maintain Productivity throughout the Year

The term "long-season breeder" refers to a breed of chicken that thrives during the longer days of the year. In other words, they begin laying eggs as soon as the number of daylight hours increases. To ensure that the chicks are able to obtain food and drink, especially water, they are kept on a light schedule of 23 to 24 hours each day for the first few days of their lives. Reducing light exposure after that time period is recommended. Just 8 hours of light a day can be given to the birds if they are being raised indoors. If you're going to expose them to the elements outside, you're going to be constrained by the number of daylight hours available to you. Increase light exposure gradually to 14 hours each day when the pullets are ready to begin laying. This exposure is expected to induce the flock to mate.

At least 14 hours of light each day must be maintained to keep the flock in a state of ovulation year-round. Late in the egg production cycle, you can gradually increase the quantity of light to 16 hours each day to help keep the flock productive. For the majority of flock owners, this technique entails the installation of additional light sources. Stop/start timers for lights can be used in the early morning before dawn and in the late evening before dusk to give the flock 14–16 hours of light exposure. Additionally, a light sensor can be purchased to ensure that the lightbulb does not turn on when the room is naturally lit. You can reduce your energy use by using this device. You don't have to use a lot of light in order to get the job done. Small flocks of chickens require 60-watt incandescent bulbs.

Nutrition

Any breed or age of chicken needs a well-rounded diet. All of a flock's nutritional requirements are met in a single package by feed mills, which combine the available ingredients. A major problem might arise if a bird is fed scratch grains plus a more expensive feed, as this can lead to nutrient depletion. It is possible for nutritional deficits to have a negative impact on pullet growth and output. It's also critical to feed your hens the right type of grain for their age and breed.

Avoid feeding a "meat-maker" style diet to chickens that are still growing or laying eggs, because it will not provide them with the nutrients they need. Chickens in the process of growing should not be fed a layer diet either. For eggshell production, the diet of a laying hen must be high in calcium. Non-laying chickens, on the other hand, are harmed by this dose of calcium. Depending on the breed, some chickens have a greater need for calcium. It's usually a good idea to have an extra calcium source on hand. Oyster shell, which can be found in most feed stores, is a good source of calcium for poultry.

Space Allowances

Laying hens require appropriate space to thrive. The size of the flock and the kind of housing determine how much floor space is needed for a flock of chickens to live comfortably. There should be at least 1.5 square feet of space for each hen, with 2 square feet of space being the most commonly used floor space needed for a flock of chickens to live comfortably. Hens that are a little bigger than average will require larger allowances. Perches can be used to maximize the space in a housing complex. At night, the hens will sleep on the perches, which will keep them off the floor and prevent them from scratching it.

Additionally, the use of perches helps reduce the amount of excrement scattered throughout the hen house. Furthermore, allowing chickens to perch is beneficial to their well-being. The quality of the outdoor environment determines how much outdoor space you'll need if you're keeping hens. Maintaining a pasture will necessitate a larger plot of land than would be required for a backyard flock with limited access to the outdoors. For easy outside access, a minimum of 2 square feet per head is often advised. If your flock has access to the outdoors, stay on the lookout for predators on the ground as well as in the air, and make sure the hens have the protection they need.

A Guide to Identifying Laying Hens

You need to know what kind of chickens you have to figure out which ones are laying. The huge red combs and wattles that are present on the hens of various breeds indicate that they are in the process of laying eggs. During the laying time, the combs and wattles of other breeds have normal color, but after the laying period, the color fades. To determine the stage of production, look at the level of yellow pigmentation on the skin of hens like Rhode Island Reds and Plymouth Rocks. In a precise sequence, hens lose their golden pigment. The vent loses its color first, followed by the head (including the beak, eye ring, and earlobe), and finally, the legs and toes (shanks, toes, and hock). The more eggs a hen will lay, the less fat she has and the more room she has in her abdomen.

Reasons Why Hens Stop Laying

The health of the hen (both before and after she lays her eggs) is one of several factors that can influence egg output. By answering these questions, you may be able to determine what is causing your hens to stop laying:

Have the chickens been laying for at least 10 months? It is inevitable that your chickens will cease to lay eggs once their laying cycle has concluded. After a molt (loss of feathers), they'll take a break, then resume their laying schedule. It's possible that your hens aren't laying because they haven't been doing so for more than 10 months.

How much clean, fresh water do the hens get? Make sure your watering system is working properly so that the hens can drink. In the winter, maintaining a watering system can be difficult because the water may freeze. It is possible to acquire waterers with built-in heaters to prevent the water from freezing. If you don't break up any frozen water, you'll have to do it on a regular basis. Issues can arise even at the height of the summer. High temperatures can cause water to become too hot for chickens to drink in the summer.

What kind of food are the chickens consuming? It's possible that providing improper feed, diluting feed with scratch grains, or restricting how much feed is available will result in a nutritional shortfall in your chickens. Feather pecking and decreased egg production are classic signs of a hen's nutritional insufficiency.

Can you tell how many hours of sunlight the hens receive every day? A flock is usually forced to go out of business when the amount of daylight falls over the day. During the fall and winter months, many flocks stop producing because they lack additional lighting.

Is there anything wrong with the hens? Poultry flocks can be infested by a variety of parasites, both internal and external. Having a large number of parasites in the digestive tract can have a negative impact on hen productivity. Anemia in chickens can result from heavy mite infestations, which can also have a negative impact on their productivity.

Is eggshell quality a factor in why egg manufacturing was stopped? Eggshell abnormalities can be caused by a variety of disorders.

Has the flock been affected by any health issues? Compared with flocks that have not been exposed to illness, those that have been sick will perform worse.

Factors Affecting Poultry Egg Production

Egg production is influenced by numerous factors, both directly and indirectly. To find out more about these aspects, we'll have to dig into the history of hens. Factors that influence egg production include age, nutrient intake, water use, light quality, light intensity and duration, and a variety of illnesses.

In the egg industry, the problem of aging hens is a major one. Longevity is not an issue for hens, as they lay eggs nonstop for their entire lifespan. A sudden decrease in egg production occurs after a few years, like 2 or 3 years. The quality of the chickens you're raising is a major factor in this. In general, good hens lay eggs for 50–60 weeks before taking a break. The term "molt" refers to the process that occurs throughout this time period. It is more common for poor and elderly hens to molt and lay eggs less frequently.

An unbalanced diet deficient in protein and calcium will reduce a chicken's ability to lay eggs to their maximum potential for only a limited time. Hens can cease laying eggs if they are fed incorrectly. The production of eggs can be reduced if protein, energy, and calcium levels are out of whack. To ensure a steady supply of eggs, it is critical to feed a well-balanced diet on a regular basis.

Many health issues, including oviductal prolapse, can be caused by an imbalanced diet. It's more common when the hens are overly fat or the eggs are overly large. Hens suffering from prolapse may suffer long-term consequences.

In addition to depriving your hens of essential nutrients, this can also reduce the frequency with which they lay eggs.

All animals, including humans, necessitate salt. The production of eggs will be reduced if salt is removed from the hens' food. Sodium chloride is the most common form of salt in an animal's diet. Iodine is not present in this product.

Maintaining the right osmotic relationship and blood pH is an important duty of sodium, which is an important nutrient. Chlorine is a crucial component as well, helping keep bodily fluids in a healthy osmotic balance. HCl, which is secreted by the stomach, assists digestion.

Calcium carbonate makes up the majority of the eggshell in laying chickens. Calcium requirements for new hens are minimal while they are growing, but as they begin to lay eggs, their calcium requirements increase by a factor of roughly four. Egg production will be reduced if there is not enough calcium in the diet. Calcium is a nutrient that can be obtained from food.

Calcium can be found in limestone. Your hens can eat it as part of their regular diet.

Vitamin D: Calcium absorption necessitates the presence of vitamin D. If the dietary item does not contain the necessary amount of vitamin D, this will have a negative impact on egg production.

To gain enough protein, birds must ingest the amino acids that makeup proteins. The body's protein contains roughly 22 different types of amino acids, all of which are necessary. It's not possible for hens to generate all of them or produce enough to suit their needs. As a result, chicken growers must supplement the food they provide with additional protein. When it comes to amino acids, there is no one-size-fits-all answer.

Egg production can be negatively affected by management faults. Some common mistakes made by farmers include the following:

Running low on food. The egg output of your chickens will decrease if you restrict their access to food. The amount of time a hen goes without nourishment affects egg output. Make sure your birds have a sufficient amount of food.

Lack of water. It's important to remember that water is a crucial component. Approximately 70% of the body's weight is water. Additionally, a lack of water can affect egg production. When it comes to a bird's well-being, water is far more vital than food.

Improper daylight and light intensity. Egg production is also influenced by the amount of daylight available. At least 14 hours of daylight are required for hens. To improve egg production, the light intensity must be sufficient.

How can you increase your poultry's egg production?

Egg and broiler birds can be produced on the floor at the same time. When producing viable eggs in commercial birds, this technique is employed. To aid in their egg production, the birds are housed in a room with a roof over their heads. However, in this manner, we would be unable to make full use of the coop. In addition, collecting and cleaning eggs is a difficult task. When it comes to raising hens for egg production, you must follow the steps outlined below to ensure that your chickens will produce the most eggs possible.

Provide for basic needs.

Food

You must provide daily nutrient units, protein, carbs, vitamins, and minerals to keep your flock healthy. The laying hens' daily diet must contain 16 to 18% protein and 3% calcium in order to maintain their health and produce eggs with a thick shell. Many poultry farmers save money by feeding their birds scraps and leftovers from their own kitchens. It significantly reduces the number of eggs produced.

Water

For optimum egg production, fresh and clean water must be available at all times. Water makes up half of the egg's volume as well as the hen's body. Inadequate fresh water supplies will limit egg production. Having a steady water supply is therefore essential, regardless of whether it is hot or dry outside.

Clean the coop

The conditions in which you raise your poultry are critically important. It is imperative that you minimize overcrowding and that you keep the area as clean as possible. In addition, visitors to your farm should not be allowed, and if they must come, they should shower before they do so.

Provide nest boxes

You must encourage your birds to lay eggs where you want them to in order to acquire clean, unbroken eggs. You don't want the hens to deposit their eggs in a random part of the coop! You can either buy a pre-made nest box from a poultry supply company, or you can design and build your own if you prefer. A layer of non-toxic wood shavings or similar soft litter should be used to line the bottom of the boxes. Even so, we recommend that you get a poultry battery cage as well as an automatic egg collection system if your farm is large. There are many hungry chickens out there, and one can teach the other how to eat eggs. So don't allow this to become a habit for them. Because most chickens stop laying at around 10 a.m., it is important to know exactly when to gather the eggs.

Set an artificial light source

The amount of light in a room can also have a significant impact on egg production. Light exposure of 14 hours is required for optimal egg production. Due to a lack of light and intensity, hens' egg production decreases throughout the winter months. Installing an artificial light source and ensuring that it is bright enough for 14 hours a day will help. The pace at which eggs are produced can be increased.

Clean the eggs

Your bird's eggs will stay clean for a long time if you collect their eggs frequently and keep their coops and nest boxes dry, clean, and uncovered. A clean egg does not need to be washed again, as it will lose the invisible layer of protection. If there is only a tiny amount of dirt, you can follow these steps:

- Dry-cleaning the eggs is as simple as using fine-grit sandpaper and a hair dryer.

- Weight washing can be used. Bacteria can enter the eggs, though, if the procedure is not carried out correctly.

- Keep the eggs away from odiferous items.

You can harvest eggs from a small layer flock in a short period of time if you know what you're looking for.

What are the telltale signs of a laying hen?

To figure out which chickens are laying eggs, you must first figure out what kind of hens you're keeping. In several varieties, egg-laying chickens have big red combs and wattles on their combs and necks. During the egg-laying period in some breeds, the chickens' combs and wattles appear normal but diminish following the egg-laying season. In the case of hens like Plymouth Rocks and Rhode Island Reds, the yellow tint in their skin serves as an excellent indicator of their current laying cycle. This arrangement is followed by the birds as they lose their color pigments. This happens first in the vents and then gradually in the face and finally in the feet.

As an alternative means of distinguishing between egg-laying and non-egg-laying hens, one can determine whether or not a hen is in the process of laying eggs by measuring how far apart the keel and pubic bones are from each other.

Why Do Hens Quit Laying Eggs?

Hens not laying eggs might be due to a variety of factors. The following question can help you discover why your hens aren't laying eggs:

How long, on average, do your hens lay eggs? Have they been laying eggs for a few months, or even a year? You should be aware that your hens might be nearing the end of their laying cycle if you answered "yes" to this question. Sometime between a few months to a year, your hens will stop laying eggs and undergo a molt. Afterward, they will begin producing eggs again. However, if the response is "no," then you need to make an inquiry to find out what is preventing production.

Is there enough potable water available? The hens won't eat if they don't have access to water. So you have to make sure that you have a suitable watering system for your chickens. Your irrigation system must be active at all times. When the water freezes, it can be a difficult chore for you. Waterers with heaters are available for purchase. Water will not freeze because of this. Summer isn't immune to problems, either. If the temperature gets too high, the hens will stop drinking water.

Are the hens getting the proper nutrition? Because they're fed the incorrect stuff and aren't getting enough food, your hens will go broody. Their egg production will be reduced as a result of frequent molting.

Do you have adequate illumination? Egg production is influenced directly by light. Your chickens will produce less if you don't give them enough light. The pace of production can only be increased by providing enough light.

Do you have hens with parasites on them? The production rate might be affected by both internal and exogenous parasites. That's why you need to exercise caution.

Tips for Increasing Egg Production

Good breeding is the first step in increasing egg production.

Using the Hogan approach has been used for decades as a way to evaluate the potential of young stock and the long-term performance of production birds. This is a reasonably simple way to teach but a time-consuming one that necessitates the evaluation of each bird by hand. Poor performers and sick or damaged birds should be removed from the laying flock on a regular basis. Feedstuffs are only going to the birds who will get the most nutritional and monetary value out of them. Just like the breeders of superb Hereford cattle or blooded horses, egg producers must take breed selection and performance enhancement as seriously as these other animal breeders. Your flock's problems with laying performance can be solved if they are dominated by roosters, you have hens older than 2 years old, you have at least one of each breed listed in a big hatchery catalog, or only raccoons and foxes cull your flock. A successful egg producer must also be a good poultry breeder in order to ensure long-term viability and consistent performance. Note on ordering chicks: The price of a well-bred pullet chick can currently run as high as $7 per bird. Many adult breeding bird trios (one male and two females) have recently been listed for $75 to $100 or more.

Increasing Egg Production by Including Feed

Chickens need a well-thought-out dietary plan at every stage of their lives, from hatching to maturity. Layer feeding should never be compromised. Hens only eat a tiny quantity of feed each day, so their diets must be high in nutrients and uniform in composition. An adult hen's daily calorie intake ranges from 4 to 8 ounces, depending on her size and the quality of her eggs. Those looking to cut feed expenses should start with birds that lay eggs in a manner that is as feed-efficient as possible. To accomplish this, the egg producer must keep track of the amount of feed she uses to create a dozen eggs. Recently, there has been some discussion about several unusual poultry ration formulas. There are a few places where customers can afford to pay a premium to offset the additional expense of certain feed ingredients. Some of these formulations might be extremely pricey.

Parts may be difficult to obtain and may need to be purchased in quantities as little as 1 to 3 tons for particularly designed diets. The old rule of thumb was that a farmer needed to produce at least 100 tons of feed per year to purchase processing equipment on the farm. The modern livestock age has been defined by steady advances in the quality of poultry rations. Rations for newborn chicks and laying hens were often the first to benefit from new knowledge of nutrition. Some of the major feed providers now offer chicken feeds that are 100% vegetarian feeds that are supplemented with omega-3 fatty acids and rations that include kelp and fish meal.

The following are some of the most important features of poultry feeding:

As a starting point, get a high-quality chick starter in limited quantities to ensure the freshness of your supply. Rations for young chickens that are designed to be fed until they produce their first eggs are common today. Both the frame and the egg tract are developed using these high-quality meals. The young females should gradually be switched to a high-quality laying diet after the first eggs develop. Certain farmers still offer young hens hard-boiled eggs, finely chopped, a practice that dates back to the 1800s. For the sake of wholesomeness, chicks should be fed no more finely chopped eggs than they can eat in 20 minutes or so at each feeding. Chicks that have had a difficult shipping experience or are otherwise anxious can benefit from this method. In a short period of time, they should be moved to a free-choice beginning ratio.

Small or mini pellet laying rations might assist in cutting down on feed waste. Birds are more likely to eat the food they flip out of a feeder if the pellets are small enough.

For optimal ration freshness and cost distribution throughout the course of the year, feedstuffs should be purchased at least every 2 weeks.

Feedstuffs should be secured from pests and humidity once they have been brought home. More than 300 pounds of feed can fit in a 55-gallon barrel.

The majority of complete poultry diets are now fortified with minerals and grit, which are essential for poultry health. Many people believe that oyster shells are good for chickens. However, they are sometimes supplied in containers that are too big for the hens to use. The sand should be dumped into low-sided wooden bins that are easily accessible to the birds. You may get high-quality grit at an affordable price by using the suitable cherry granite grit size.

In many modern feeding systems, scratch grain is no longer necessary. Egg production may decrease if birds consume too much grain, which they refer to as the full diet that helps them lay more eggs. Grain should only be given out once or twice a day, at the end of the day when the birds are returning home from their day's foraging. With this extra burst of energy, the birds are ready for the cold winter nights ahead.

Many farmers continue to provide expensive feedstuffs to birds that cannot use them, despite the fact that you can't get as many eggs from old hens or those bred for other purposes.

When it comes to food and seed stock, decreasing costs is never an option.

Increasing egg production can be as simple as making sure the hens have access to clean water and food. As producers gain expertise, they will be able to identify which birds need to be replaced, when to do so, and how to improve the breed of replacement birds.

Egg Production May be Slowed in Stressful Situations

Reduce the amount of anxiety your chickens are experiencing to the absolute minimum. Egg production can be affected by seasonal stressors. Extensive bouts of wind and heat can have a devastating effect on egg production in the Southwest. Even short-term cold outbreaks can have a significant impact on egg production. When their birds need a little more help, seasoned producers have a variety of tactics up their sleeves:

During these stressful periods, an increase in protein intake may be beneficial. With a higher crude protein level, some farmers supplement their hens' regular diet with some of the game bird breeding feed. Preferably, the crude protein content of the egg-laying ration should be in the 18–20% range. Many generic lying mashes have a maximum of just 16%.

You can give the birds a small amount of green food by using a simple mesh feeder positioned just above the birds' heads to provide leafy legume hay. Collards, for example, can be held above the birds in the same way as the stalks of green crops. Birds who have been cooped up can get some exercise by participating in this practice. It's also a good idea to feed alfalfa hay every few days to help maintain healthy yolk color and to increase fertility.

Use an electrolyte or vitamin supplement in the water during times of stress.

Producers can add a variety of appetite-stimulating or tonic-type ingredients to drinking water. These can range from basic mixtures of red pepper, garlic, and oregano to a vast spectrum of commercial boosters.

Keep birds free of parasites that might sabotage their performance.

Adding a few ribbons of wheat germ or cod liver oil to the laying feed several times a week is an old-fashioned method for keeping chickens warm in the winter.

The hens' breeding, feeding, and care are critical to the success and profitability of egg production. No matter what scale you're working at, I believe these suggestions will help you sustainably and inexpensively boost your laying rates.

8

CHICKEN EGGS: HOW TO COLLECT AND CLEAN THEM?

Take a look at the wet and dry cleaning techniques. Whether you're keeping chickens for your own household or planning to sell eggs at a local farmers market, quality and safety should always be your top priorities. It's important to know how to clean eggs correctly after collecting them. The welfare of the chickens, the eggs, and the people who eat them all depend on the procedures you employ.

The Proper Method for Gathering Eggs

You need to collect the eggs first, then clean them. Broody hens are responsible for incubating eggs, so it's important to have certain equipment and knowledge on hand when raising chickens. To reduce the time spent cleaning, it is best to select eggs that are as fresh and clean as possible. Try to gather eggs as soon as possible after they have been laid or as early in the day as possible. You can keep chicken eggs cleaner if you gather them two or three times a day. It stops a hen from brooding and keeps the chickens from consuming the eggs (never leaving the eggs). Leaving eggs in the nest boxes overnight might cause them to get soiled with excrement or break.

It might appear that some of the chickens like to roost in or near the nesting boxes. Overnight, they can poop on the eggs that are left in the cartons or step on them and break the shells. As a general rule, if you miss a day of egg collection, you'll have to make up for it the next day. Feathered nest boxes are another important maintenance task. Put plenty of shavings or straw in the chickens' nesting boxes. The nest boxes should be thoroughly cleaned of any feces before the eggs are removed and new straw or shavings should be put in their place. For the same reason, once an egg has been broken, the coop must be completely cleaned, including the removal of any damp or filthy straw. Regular maintenance must be performed to increase the likelihood of hens using the nest boxes.

How to Clean Eggs

By learning the appropriate way to clean eggs, you can protect yourself, your loved ones, and potential buyers from food poisoning. Chicken eggs can be cleaned in two fundamental ways: dry and moist. If you want to avoid refrigerating your eggs, dry cleaning is the way to go because it preserves the eggs' natural antibacterial protective covering, known as the bloom. Eggs can be "dry cleaned" by wiping them with a loofah, an abrasive sponge, or even fine sandpaper to get rid of any remaining dirt and excrement. Wet cleaning may be required if eggs are particularly unclean or if the yolk has adhered to the shells. The best way to clean eggs is in a running sink using warm water. The water temperature needs to be warmer than the egg temperature but not hot. Eggs should be dried with a paper towel and stored in a clean, open carton or wire rack. Spraying the cleaned eggs with a bleach and water mixture is an effective way to disinfect them. If you want to sell your eggs, you should find out the local and state laws regarding the preparation of eggs for sale by contacting your county extension office.

Tips for Storing Eggs

Once the eggs have been washed and dried, they should be placed in egg cartons and dated to indicate when they were gathered. Eggs should be refrigerated for maximum freshness and longevity. Eggs that have been wet-cleaned must be refrigerated, but eggs that have been dry-cleaned (with the bloom still intact) can be stored at room temperature or in the refrigerator. Refrigeration extends the shelf life of eggs regardless of their type.

Some guidelines for the care and storage of eggs are as follows:

When refrigerated, eggs can be eaten for up to 5 weeks after they are gathered. Even after a month, the eggs might be fine to eat for another 2 or 3 weeks. You can use older eggs for baking or hard boiling. Dry-cleaned eggs can be stored at room temperature for around a week, but they must be thoroughly washed before cooking.

The Quality of Fresh Eggs

If you want to know if your eggs are still okay to eat, use the float test. Drop the eggs into a dish of water. If an egg floats, the contents have evaporated too much, leaving a large air pocket inside the shell, and the egg is likely spoiled. Use it in a compost pile. An additional method, known as candling, uses a bright light to reveal the volume of air within an egg.

9

THE MOST FREQUENT CHICKEN HEALTH ISSUES

This section may have the answer to why your feathered pals are acting strangely or looking sad. As a chicken keeper, you should be aware of a few frequent health problems with chickens.

Broody Hens

When a hen gets broody, she may refuse to leave the nest box, even if she knows the eggs within are unfertilized. Broodiness in chickens is more common in the summer but can occur at any time of year. Some chickens may have a strong maternal instinct that drives them to try to hatch eggs regardless of whether or not they are fertilized, but the actual origin of broodiness in hens remains a mystery. Cochins and Silkies, for example, are more likely to develop broodiness than other breeds.

Signs of a Broody Hen

You can tell when you have a broody hen because she will exhibit drastic changes in her behavior. You will likely initially observe that you are dealing with a particularly sour hen. The symptoms of a broody hen are as follows:

- She is unwilling to leave the nesting box.
- She fluffs her feathers to make herself appear larger.
- When you attempt to remove her, she starts growling and pecking.
- When removed, she returns to the nesting box.
- She plucks her chest feathers.

When a hen becomes broody, what can be done about it?

There are a few different ways to handle a broody hen. A few of these strategies entail either working with her broodiness or simply accepting it. There are several methods for "brooding out" a hen that are more effective than others. Following are a few of these methods.

Leaving Her

A broody hen will remain so for around the 3 weeks it takes to incubate eggs. It's up to you whether you want to intervene or just let nature take its course. It's important to give her a break from the nest box for a few hours every day and provide her food and water while you're at it. Even if she does take up the nesting box, the other hens will likely be fine with sharing it with her. However, if you have a broody hen that is very hostile, she may peck at the other hens if they try to lay an egg in the same nesting box. When you know that all the other hens in the coop have produced their eggs, you may want to lock your broody hen outside. Because a broody hen is likely to get violent if she is forcibly removed from her nest, it is recommended that you wear protective gloves if you decide to do so.

Acquire Some Fertilized Eggs

Making use of a hen that goes broody is essential if you want to hatch eggs and raise your own chicks. As opposed to using an incubator, hatching eggs with a hen is simple and requires no extra equipment. Everything from incubation to raising to learning the ropes as chicks are handled by the hen. If you're new to keeping chickens, it's smart to consult an expert.

Submersing Her Bottom in Water

A chicken's body temperature rises when she becomes broody. The goal is to bring down her body temperature and thereby alleviate her brooding. Broody hens can be cured by immersing their feet in a pail of ice water. Nonetheless, there is debate amongst poultry keepers as to whether or not this technique is actually beneficial, given that it typically serves as a distraction while she dries herself. This method is only advised during the hotter summer months.

Putting Cold Packs or Frozen Peas Underneath Her

This is another attempt to get her to a more comfortable temperature in the nesting box, but it will also make her uncomfortable.

Creating a Broody Enclosure

Put your broody hen in a wire cage or dog box with food and water. The wire cage will make her uncomfortable and possibly cause her to stop brooding by reducing the temperature in her chest and vent area. There is no set time frame for how long it will take a particular hen to stop being broody. In most cases, 3 days will suffice. When a hen is no longer broody, she will stop fluffing her feathers and won't rush back to the nest after being let out. Although this may seem cruel, it may be better for her health in the long term than letting her sit in an empty nest.

Egg-Bound Hens

When an egg is unable to pass through the cloaca from the uterus to the outside of the body, the hen is said to be "egg-bound." The hen will make valiant attempts to expel the egg but will ultimately fail. If egg binding is not diagnosed and treated in hens, it can be lethal.

Symptoms and Signs

- The hen will come and go from the nest without depositing an egg.

- She will walk with her bottom almost touching the ground, like a penguin.

- She will appear droopy.

- She may not be eating or drinking.

- She will have a hard abdomen.

You should check to determine if a hen is egg-bound if you see any of these signs. Start by feeling her lower abdomen for a round, egg-shaped mass. She is probably egg-bound if you feel an egg.

Treatment

A warm bath is the standard therapy for a hen that has become egg-bound. This will help relax the hen's muscles and facilitate the passage of the egg. Don't delay in taking your hen to the vet if a warm bath doesn't help her pass the egg.

Hen Pecking, Cannibalism, and Mistreatment

Hens can become extremely aggressive when they see blood or red wounds, which can be unpleasant for anyone who has chickens. Sometimes this leads to chickens picking at each other's feathers and, in the worst cases, cannibalism that kills them all. A flock may exhibit this behavior for a variety of reasons. Lack of room is the most common cause of pecking among chickens. They may become anxious and start pecking at one another or bullying a chicken lower in the pecking order as a result. Giving them some breathing room may help if you suspect this is the case.

You should also hang food from the ceiling or provide other exciting distractions for their run. Removing the offending hen from the flock for a few days may assist; she will be at the bottom of the hierarchical order when she is reintroduced and should therefore desist from her past violent conduct. Your other chickens may start pecking at a sick hen, especially if she has a wound. Chickens are known to relentlessly peck at any red wound they come across. A healthy chicken can be reintroduced to the flock after a period of isolation, but a sick one must be removed and kept away from the others until it has fully recovered.

Adding New Birds to the Coop

There will always be some pecking and bullying when you introduce a new chicken to the group. It is only logical that they do this when establishing a pecking order. There shouldn't be any prolonged pecking like this. Even though chickens can be cruel, you shouldn't step in until you're sure a fowl is in danger of being gravely hurt. It is possible to stop the pecking of a single hen whose aggression is generating problems. There's a chance you'll have to do this several times before she stops harassing the new hen.

Crop Impaction or Blockage

At the very bottom of the esophagus is a pouch known as the crop. It is responsible for the first few steps of digestion. If this becomes clogged, food will accumulate internally. If a chicken's crop is affected, however, it will not empty at night, and the chicken will have to be slaughtered.

Symptoms of Crop Impaction or Blockage

A chicken with a crop obstruction will show signs of illness and indifference toward food and water consumption, as well as the inability to defecate or the presence of loose, watery feces. If this problem isn't fixed, the chicken will start to lose weight. If a chicken has a blocked crop, it will take some time before it eats in the morning, but it will still have a full crop when it wakes up. Although long, thick, or dead grass is often at fault, any number of things might obstruct a drain. If your chicken has a minor case of a blocked crop, you can try massaging the crop with warm water or vegetable oil to release whatever is stuck inside and give it a drink. If it doesn't help and your chicken's crop feels really hard and compacted, it's time to visit the vet. Under local anesthesia, the veterinarian will empty the crop. Try to keep the grass your chickens graze on short to avoid a clogged crop.

Soft-Shelled Eggs

Hens can lay eggs even if there is no shell. Therefore, shelled eggs aren't the only kind. Soft-shelled eggs are terribly lopsided. They will often be shattered before you even get to them due to how readily they break. Hybrid chickens produce soft-shelled eggs more often than any other type of chicken.

The occasional soft-shelled egg is very normal and should not cause any alarm. However, if you notice one of your hens consistently lays eggs that are too soft or lack a shell, you need to investigate her diet. The absence of calcium in the diet is the most prevalent cause of soft-shelled eggs.

The eggshells of hens depend on calcium for 95% of their composition, so providing them with plenty of calcium is essential. To make sure they get enough calcium, feed them grit that contains oyster shells. Your chickens will eat as much as they need if you provide a steady supply.

There's a chance that the hens' soft eggshells are the result of your giving them too many table scraps. Your hens will consume fewer layer pellets, the source of the protein and calcium they need to grow and lay eggs, if you give them rewards. Stress from other health issues can cause the eggshell to become soft.

Parasites and illnesses are examples. If giving your hens more calcium and fewer treats doesn't solve the problem, then you should observe them closely to determine the underlying cause.

Rare Chicken Diseases

Chickens, like people, will occasionally get sick and require special care from their owners. As a chicken keeper, you will eventually come across a sad, sagging hen. Chickens aren't great at concealing their discomfort, so if there is an issue, you'll likely notice it very quickly. This section will go over the signs and symptoms of the more prevalent chicken diseases.

Coccidiosis

The culprit of coccidiosis is a small parasitic bug that has taken up residence in your hens' intestinal lining. An infected chicken might experience excruciating discomfort due to damage to the lining of its digestive tract. Because of how badly it affects the bird's digestive system, it can be lethal if left untreated. Coccidiosis vaccinations are routinely given by reputable breeders prior to selling their birds.

Symptoms

Diarrhea containing blood/ Obesity/ Sad and ill appearance/ Reduction in egg production

Treatment

In order to treat coccidiosis infection, anticoccidial medicines such as Toxoid are used. Coccidiosis causes bacterial disturbances in the gut and may necessitate antibiotic treatment to alleviate the symptoms. To prevent your chickens from ingesting any more oocysts, you will need to treat the area where they live. Every day, you can give your chickens a new experience by moving their coop and running to a new location. To prevent illness, you should use a ground sanitizer to clean the area around their static run. You should consult a veterinarian if you suspect coccidial disease in your chickens.

Mycoplasma

Mycoplasmas are unusual among bacteria in that they lack a cell wall that surrounds their membrane. Mycoplasma gallisepticum is the most widespread strain of Mycoplasma, but there are many more. Respiratory infections brought on by Mycoplasma are often lethal. It is true that many birds can catch Mycoplasma and pull through unscathed. A stressed bird that already carries the virus is at risk of having it flare up again.

All new birds with weakened immune systems are at risk of becoming unwell and eventually dying if there is a carrier in the flock. Seeing as the disease can be spread by wild birds, free-range hens are at a higher risk of contracting it.

Symptoms

Bubbling or fluid accumulation in the eye's periphery/ A drop in egg production/ Swollen face with sweet-smelling breath/ Coughing/ Sneezing/ Nasal discharge. Mycoplasma can survive on the surfaces of drinkers, feeders, and clothing for a number of hours, making it extremely contagious.

Treatment

Antibiotic medication is the standard treatment. Consult your veterinarian for a diagnosis and treatment of Mycoplasma in hens if you suspect the disease.

Colibacillosis

A bacterial infection caused by the bacteria *E. coli* is called colibacillosis. In severe cases, it is linked to pneumonia, but in most cases, the chicken will make a full recovery. Colibacillosis is most common in birds between the ages of 5 and 6 weeks but can affect birds of any age.

Symptoms

Listlessness/ Labored breathing/ Reduced appetite/ Ruffled feathers/ Coughing/ Sneezing. Veterinarians are the best resource for information and treatment options for birds exhibiting any of the aforementioned symptoms, so don't hesitate to get in touch if you see any problems.

Treatment

Antibiotic medication is the standard treatment.

Fowl Cholera

Cholera in chickens is a bacterial disease. Chronic infections tend to be mild, and although the birds will recover, they will always be carriers. Similarly, birds can contract acute chicken cholera, which can be fatal in a matter of hours even if no outward signs have developed. Because rodents play a role in the transmission of this disease, reducing their numbers is a good way to curb its spread. Some farmers have decided to cull infected birds to stop the spread of the disease.

Symptoms

Swollen wattles/ Chronic twisting of the neck/ Swollen joints/ Mucus coming out of the beak/ Sudden death.

Get in touch with your veterinarian right away if your birds have any of the aforementioned symptoms.

Treatment

Antibiotic tetracyclines. Once a chicken has the disease, it will never recover.

Fowl Pox

The virus that causes fowl pox can be transferred by a variety of vectors, including mosquitoes, the wind, and open sores. It's not lethal, but it hurts your chickens a lot. Both a "wet" and a "dry" form exist, with the latter being the more common. Suffocation is a common outcome for birds with the "wet" type.

Poultry relapsing fever is simple to diagnose but has no effective treatment. This virus has a vaccine, but most poultry keepers don't bother with it because it kills so few birds.

Symptoms

A drop in egg production/ Cheese-like caseous deposits in the oral cavity and the pharynx (only in the wet form)/ Scabs on wattles, and combs/ Loss of appetite

Treatment

No specific treatment exists at this time. The incubation period for this illness is about 3–5 weeks. If you want your chickens to get better, give them some apple cider vinegar or a vitamin booster. If you are concerned that your chickens may have fowlpox, it is best to consult a veterinarian.

Infectious Bronchitis

One of the most prevalent viral diseases affecting hens' upper respiratory systems is infectious bronchitis (IB). Hobby chicken keepers shouldn't have to worry about this if their hens are vaccinated because most hybrid chickens are protected against many strains. Considering how contagious IB is, it's probable that it will swiftly infect the entire flock. Birds younger than 5 weeks old have a significant mortality rate. Most mature birds make a full recovery in a few weeks.

Symptoms

Sneezing/ Coughing/ Wet litter/ Gasping/ Diarrhea/ Loss of appetite/ Smaller, soft-shelled eggs with irregular shapes. Chickens displaying any of these signs should be taken straight to the vet.

Treatment

Like other viral illnesses, there is currently no cure. A veterinarian may recommend antibiotics to help control an existing bacterial infection or to stop the spread of bacteria.

Your chickens will benefit from apple cider vinegar or a vitamin booster, both of which have been shown to be effective against fowl pox.

Infectious Laryngotracheitis

There are viruses that can cause infectious laryngitis. There are exceptions, but generally speaking, it doesn't end in death. Typical mortality ranges from 10% to 20%, with rates as high as 50% being recorded.

A bird can continue to carry the virus for the rest of its life after a typical 6-week course of treatment. Even though the virus is resistant and may live for a long period away from its host, it is readily eliminated by using disinfectants. By frequently disinfecting the coop and run, you can reduce the likelihood that your chickens may catch this disease.

Symptoms

Shortness of breath/ Coughing with or without phlegm or blood/ Gasping/ Eye and nasal discharge / A drop in egg production. displaying any of these signs should be taken to a veterinarian immediately.

Treatment

This virus cannot be cured. In the event that the chicken develops a secondary bacterial illness due to its weaker immune system, your veterinarian may prescribe medications to treat it.

Sour Crop

A yeast infection causes sour fruit. A chicken's crop is a pouch at the back of the neck. This process is the initial step in breaking down food. The infection causes the wall of the crop to thicken, blocking the crop. Starvation can be fatal if not handled properly. Birds that are still young are more likely to develop sour crops than mature birds. Some oral antibiotics or a deficiency in vitamin A may bring it on in your chickens.

Symptoms

Foul breath/ Looking droopy and deflated/ A drop in egg production/ Loss of weight

Treatment

Taking your chicken to the vet is probably your best bet. The chicken's crop will be emptied and cleaned by the vet, who will then likely prescribe anti-fungal medicine to reduce bacterial growth in the crop.

Egg Peritonitis

When the ovary releases the yolk, it goes into the abdominal cavity rather than the oviduct; this is called "egg peritonitis." Your chicken's health is in danger as the virus spreads. Most of the time, by the time your chicken develops signs, it is already too late to save its life. Chickens have a chance of survival if they are found early. It can be difficult to make a diagnosis if a chicken shows no signs of illness before it dies. Here are a few indicators to keep an eye out for.

Symptoms

Pale comb and wattles/ Lack of appetite/ Penguin stance/ A lack of expression/ A sluggish appearance/ A failure to eat or drink/ A drop in egg production

Treatment

If the infection is found early enough, antibiotics can treat it, and your chicken will get better. Unfortunately, egg peritonitis is often fatal if not treated in time to save your chickens.

Prolapsed Oviduct

When the tissues inside the vent bulge out through the vent, this is called a prolapse. Normally, this happens during the process of laying eggs. As the chicken prepares to lay an egg, the tissue around the egg will expand. Tissue that has prolapsed from the oviduct does not retract back inside. It's just as likely that a hen lays an extraordinarily huge egg as it is that a pullet will start laying before she's completely mature.

Symptoms

A strand of blood-red tissue dangling from the chicken's air duct

Treatment

Before the other hens begin to pick at the chicken, you should quickly remove her from the flock. The tissue may contract back in on its own, but most of the time, you'll need to assist it. Put the hen in a bowl of warm water and carefully scrub the vent and tissue for any dirt or poop. Gently press the tissue back inside her vent with some petroleum jelly, and then apply some Preparation H or witch hazel to bring down the swelling. The hen will need to be quarantined for a few days. Keep her in the dark so her oviduct can relax and she won't lay any eggs. She can rejoin the flock after a few days of rest, but you need to keep a watchful check on her in case she prolapses again. Take a prolapsed hen to the vet if you don't feel confident treating it yourself.

Botulism

The toxin that causes avian botulism can be swallowed or inhaled or can enter a chicken via an open wound. The toxin-producing bacteria live in decomposing organic debris like dead plants and animals. The bacteria require anaerobic (oxygen-free) conditions, a protein supply, and a heated environment in order to create the toxin. When the poison blocks nerve function, it paralyzes the muscles and makes it difficult to breathe.

Symptoms

The legs, wings, neck, and eyelids are all paralyzed, resulting in death.

Treatment

Clean up the contaminated area, such as a chicken run or coop, and remove the poison. Give the chicken selenium; vitamins A, D, and E; and maybe even some antibiotics like chlortetracycline or bacitracin. Contact your local veterinarian immediately if you suspect your chicken has botulism.

Feather Loss

Don't freak out if any of your chickens start looking a little disheveled or even bald. Your pet chickens can quickly molt and regain their feathered appearance with some tender loving care, a stress-free environment, and high-quality nutrition.

When do your chickens molt, and what does that mean?

Molting occurs once a year and is a normal and healthy part of the life cycle. The process includes removing damaged feathers and replacing them with brand-new, healthy ones. The majority of hens will molt their feathers around the end of summer, and some may even repeat the process later in the year, particularly on their necks. Although it may seem like it's taking forever, the process usually only takes around a month to a couple of months. You may be shocked at how much longer it takes your purebred chickens to molt than your hybrid hens, but we assure you that the wait is well worth it.

The Diet of Molting Chickens Must Be Balanced

Make sure your chickens get the proper quantity of vitamins and minerals because molting requires a surprising amount of energy and can tire them out. To ensure they get enough of everything they need to stay healthy during this time, you can add supplements to their diet. When a chicken is molting, it needs a high-protein diet so that its feathers can regrow.

Chickens' diets are made up of vitamins, minerals, and amino acids, all of which can be obtained in supplemental chicken vitamin forms. For optimal health during the molt, you can also supplement your chickens' diet with apple cider vinegar. Your chickens will benefit from its high mineral content and enjoy longer lives.

Avoid Stressful Situations

When your hens are in the midst of molting, it's best not to subject them to any major changes, such as a move or the introduction of new birds to the flock. It's also important to know that your hens are more susceptible to disease during the two months preceding their molt.

Why don't my chickens lay eggs anymore?

When it comes to protein content, chicken eggs and feathers rank among the highest. Most of your hens will stop laying when they start molting because they need every ounce of protein they can obtain to regrow their feathers.

10

PROTECTING CHICKENS FROM COLD AND PREDATORS

Warming Up Your Chickens

There are a number of things you can do to make sure your chickens are warm and comfortable in their coop when the weather outside becomes cold. Consider putting into practice some of the following measures to keep your chickens toasty and healthy throughout the cold season:

Put something hot in the coop, such as a ceramic heater or a heat lamp.

Extra bedding can help retain the heat in the coop longer.

As a means of keeping birds warm, you should provide them with heated perches.

Birds will need more energy to generate body heat, so be sure to provide them with plenty of food.

You should provide the birds with a heating pad so they can warm themselves as needed.

Scratch grains and other environmental enrichment should be available to keep the chickens busy.

Maintain proper ventilation for the birds' well-being while sealing any drafty sections of the coop.

Water heaters should be used to keep water supplies from freezing.

Precautions to Take When the Temperature Drops

Despite being able to thrive in milder climes, how can you detect whether your flock needs extra warmth? The following measures can be taken to increase the likelihood of healthy chickens during the winter:

Apply petroleum jelly or some similar product to prevent frostbite on combs and wattles.

To stop water from freezing, keep it de-iced by checking it twice a day. Get the containers inside for the night if frost is in the forecast, or if that's not an option, invest in a water heater made specifically for the purpose of preventing water from freezing. Freezing can also be avoided by placing ping pong balls in the waterer.

Although hens typically head back to the coop after sunset, you may notice that your winter chickens are staying out later in the day to get in more pecking. If your chickens are nocturnal scavengers, a high-visibility hen coat will not only make it easier to track them down but will also make them more noticeable to passers-by in the event that they wander away from your land or backyard. It's a win-win situation because the birds benefit from the coats too.

Heat lamps or oil-filled radiators can be used to offer supplemental heat in outbuildings, but they should only be used for birds that are particularly weak or have lost a significant number of feathers. Instead of trying to genuinely warm the environment, just make it feel a little less frigid.

If you can't afford an Eglu, you may insulate a wooden coop with bubble wrap, cardboard, or even just some old carpets and blankets to keep the hens warm.

Adding more bedding to the coop floor is another good way to keep the chickens toasty.

The chickens will appreciate a dry place to take a break from the rain in the chicken run.

If you give your hens some additional corn as a reward before bedtime, their bodies will generate heat from the maize's digestion throughout the night. In order to replenish the energy they expend keeping warm, hens typically increase their food consumption throughout the winter.

Some hen keepers supplement their hens' diets with suet or extra protein to help them gain weight before winter. The fat helps keep the warmth in, which is good for the whole bird

Tips for Preventing Chickens from Being Eaten by Predators

Make it a habit to bring your chickens back to their coop each night, and always lock the door when you're done. Chickens raised in the coop will go out throughout the day to forage for food and then come back to roost and lay eggs in the coop at night. When night falls and the birds have settled in, make sure the house is secure by locking the doors and windows.

Prevent rodents, skunks, and snakes from making the chicken coop their home and raiding your eggs, chicks, and young hens by elevating it a foot or so off the ground. Patch any gaps in the henhouse floor to prevent snakes or rodents from entering.

You should build a secure chicken run around the coop to keep off predators like coyotes, dogs, bobcats, and other canine and feline carnivores. Chicken wire, welded wire mesh, electric netting, and so on can be used as fencing if their holes are tiny enough or their electrical pulses are strong enough. Great jumpers like bobcats and coyotes may quickly clear 4-foot-high fences, so make sure your enclosure is at least that height, or cover it with a cover net.

You should take measures to protect your birds from being eaten by hawks and owls. Chicken wire, welded wire fencing, game-bird netting, or a haphazard network of crisscrossing wires can all be used to enclose the chicken run. Your chickens will be safe from nighttime owl attacks if you keep them in the coop. Don't wait until nightfall to secure the coop if owls are an issue in your area; they can be sneaky when it comes to snatching their prey.

Fencing materials with a tiny mesh size should be used to surround coops and runs when mink, raccoons, and fishers are a concern. It is common knowledge that raccoons and other nimble animals will kill hens by reaching through chicken wire or other larger-mesh fencing and strangling them. This is especially important when using a chicken tractor or similar floorless mobile coop design or when keeping chickens in a fully enclosed wire coop/run. The loss of birds can be minimized by switching from 2-by-3-inch wire fencing to 1-by-2-inch mesh or smaller welded wire.

To prevent predators from breaching your surface fencing in the chicken run, bury a welded-wire fence or galvanized hardware cloth around its perimeter.

Install a set of Nite Guard solar predator-deterrent lights or a motion-activated night light to keep your chickens safe after dark. Most nocturnal predators will avoid the coop if this is in place.

Give your dog free reign of the coop at night if it gets along well with the chickens. If you plan on letting your dogs run free in the chicken yard during the day or leaving the chicken coop open overnight, you should keep a watch on them to ensure that they do not become lured to chase after any of the scurrying and crowing chickens.

If you find predation, you should be ready to act quickly. It is possible to prevent the predator from getting to your birds or to eliminate its access to your birds altogether.

Make a perimeter around the chicken coop and yard that is impenetrable to predators. The vast majority of terrestrial predators would rather not venture into an area with such little concealment. Your chickens will appreciate some shade and a chance to nibble on some leaves if you plant some plants inside the run, but try to keep the perimeter as clear of vegetation as possible. Having to sit in the open deters raccoons from trying to use their "hands" to climb over or dig under welded-wire fencing.

Solutions to Predator Threats to Chickens

Recognizing that there is always a predator lurking around is the first step in protecting your flock against roving predators. Opossums, foxes, and raccoons may even target flocks in the suburbs. Animals will work nonstop to get to your chickens if they are really hungry.

Constructing a safe hen yard is the first step in keeping predators at bay.

Predators will avoid your hen house if you take these steps. Before ambushing, most predators want a patch of brush or some other form of shelter. In order to reduce hiding spots for potential predators, it is important to keep the space around your chickens uncluttered.

Put the coop up on stilts, so it's not touching the ground. Make sure the hen house has ramps for the chickens to use while entering and leaving.

The eggs should be gathered at least twice a day. Give animals no reason to come to your house. Simply laying eggs is a huge draw.

Enclose the entire chicken run with fencing. If you want to keep hawks and owls out of your chicken yard, build a fence or a mesh barrier over the top. To prevent predators from entering, use wire mesh no larger than 1 inch by 2 inches in size.

Train your free-range chickens to sleep in the hen house every night for their own protection. Toss a handful of grain into a container and give it a good shake before feeding it to your chickens. As soon as they learn to identify the noise with food, they'll come running.

If that is not enough to keep predators away, then other measures may be required.

When potential danger is present on your land, guard dogs or other livestock might sound the alarm. It is common practice for poultry farmers to keep a few guinea hens as avian sentries to keep an eye on the rest of the flock. When a predator is near, guinea hens will make a lot of noise. Guard dogs are effective at preventing foxes from stealing chicks if they have been trained to ignore the birds. Coyotes and raccoons are two more animals that can be driven away by a barking dog.

Nighttime pest control is simplified with motion-activated lighting. Start them up once all of your chickens are safely inside the coop. Be prepared to make a mad dash for the door if the lights come on to scare away any potential attackers. You may safely and effectively scare away predators with nothing more than a noise maker or party horn, both of which can be purchased at most department stores. The neighbors might protest if your alarm goes off too loud.

Extensions of the fencing wire a few inches down into the ground and a few inches out can prevent skunks and other predators from digging under the hen yard fence. If you want to keep predators away from your hen house, you'll need to bury the wire around its perimeter. Bury the wire and angle it so that it points away from the coop at an L-shaped angle. When predators come up against the wire, they will eventually stop digging.

11

Chicken Care Routine

Chicken Husbandry: A Guide for New and Experienced Keepers Using a Daily Checklist

It takes a lot of effort to raise a flock of chickens, but the effort is well worth it when you see the happiness on the hens' faces when you provide the things they require. Raising chickens is a skill that may be learned with little effort. In this chapter, find out about some of the fundamental responsibilities associated with keeping chickens, such as managing bedding and water and providing for them throughout the colder months. Keeping to this routine all year long will help ensure that your chickens remain healthy and productive, producing an abundance of eggs.

Activities Performed Daily When Caring for Chickens

Daily maintenance includes the following tasks:

Ensure the water is clean and replenish it if necessary. Give your chickens access to a constant supply of fresh water. Chickens won't drink unclean water and will quickly become dehydrated if they go without it. Over the course of the day, shavings, straw, and dung can find their way into the water, fouling it. If you notice any debris or sliminess in the container, you should replace the water. Regular cleanings with dish soap and water are recommended, followed by a thorough rinsing before reuse. Similarly, chlorine bleach or oxygen bleach can be used to sterilize the water container, provided that it is rinsed completely after use.

Feed the Chickens

Using a large hanging feeder, you can provide chicken feed on demand while letting your birds forage for food. You can either provide free-choice food or a predetermined amount per day.

Collect Eggs

Daily egg collection is recommended for the cleanest eggs. It's a great way to keep eggs fresh and decrease the number of broken eggs.

Observe the Chickens

Ensure the health of the hens by spending some time with them. Chickens that are active, alert, and have shiny feathers and clear eyes are positive signs.

Monthly Chicken Care Tasks

Manage the Bedding

The specifics of this process are determined by the type of trash you're employing. Bedding in the coop should be changed at least once every month for small flocks. However, the deep litter technique can be used by flocks across more expansive areas. Starting with a depth of 3–4 inches is ideal for this technique. If the droppings are piling up, or if it's been a month, add extra bedding until you have 6 inches. Then, twice a year, you should clean everything out and start fresh. Chicken manure, which is high in nitrogen, can also be composted and used in the garden.

Freshen the Nest Boxes

Whenever the nest box's bedding becomes soiled with feces or shattered eggs, remove the filthy sections and replace them with clean ones. Cleaning the nest boxes is simple, and your chickens are more likely to stay put when you do it.

Sanitize the Waterers

The water storage containers should be thoroughly scrubbed at least once a month. Put them through a sanitizing process using any method you like; the quickest and easiest is using a solution of 1 part bleach to 10 parts water. The waterers should be washed with dish soap and warm water to eliminate any built-up residue of bleach and soap before being refilled with clean water.

Tasks Twice a Year

Scrub and disinfect the chicken coop. At least twice a year, empty the coop so that you may give it a thorough cleaning using a solution of 1 part bleach to 10 parts water. You should also do this while moving between flocks or when one of your animals becomes ill. Diatomaceous earth is sometimes used to rid the coop of mites and ensure the hens stay healthy. Get some diatomaceous earth that is suitable for human consumption, and don't worry if the hens consume any of it.

Prepare for the Winter

If you want your hens to survive the winter, you need to prepare them for the cold. If you need to heat your water, you can do so. To keep your hens lying during the winter, you might want to think about using a light (to mimic sunshine). In order to keep your chickens warm, you should provide them with a place to sleep at night. However, you shouldn't warm up the chickens' coop.

12

Chicken Behavior and Psychology

Solve the Problem of Your Flock's Bad Habits

Some typical chicken behaviors and suggestions for improving them are detailed below.

Having Eggs on the Floor

Young hens, in particular, often struggle with the behavioral issue of laying eggs on the ground rather than in the nest. Without more experienced chickens there to guide them, young chicks may start laying their eggs in the wrong areas.

Why is it necessary to stop?

Eggs can be easily crushed if they are allowed to roll around on the floor unattended, so it's crucial to break this habit. Curious chickens may start pecking at the eggs, which may result in egg eating.

More hens laying eggs on the ground will lead to the other hens treating this as the norm and following suit.

How to break the habit:

One nesting box per three to four hens is a good rule of thumb, so make sure you have enough of these for your flock. This is because chickens don't all lay eggs at once, and they use communal nesting boxes.

Quickly pick up all the eggs from the floor so the other hens don't find them. So that the chickens will know where to deposit their eggs, you should: Put some dummy eggs in each nesting box.

Egg-eating

The incessant need to consume eggs is a particularly irritating behavior for a chicken to pick up. Your flock has already eaten all of your eggs before you even get a chance to collect them.

Why is it important to stop?

You can forget about having a plateful of fresh eggs for breakfast every day! Because of its infectious nature, other chickens in the flock will start eating eggs if one of them does.

Not only do they eat the eggs they lay, but they will also eat any eggs they can get their beaks on.

How to break the habit:

No magic bullets exist to save the egg-laying hens from their own gluttony. The majority of these techniques are most effective as preventative measures, but there are a few that have been shown to actually break the habit.

Ensure that each hen has a safe and comfortable place to nest. Never miss a day without collecting the day's fresh egg supply.

Incorporate shell grit into your chickens' feeds if you haven't already to ensure they get enough protein and calcium.

Put golf balls or plastic eggs in their nesting boxes to fool the chickens into thinking they're eating real eggs.

While the other birds in the flock are producing eggs, remove the problematic one and place it in temporary, secure confinement.

Roosting on the Floor

It may not seem like a big deal, but if chickens get into the habit of sleeping on the floor instead of their perch, it can lead to serious health issues. There is no greater choice than that perch.

Why is it important to stop?

It's possible that if the bedding hasn't been changed recently, they may be sleeping next to feces if the roosting area is on the floor. Droppings emit ammonia gas, which might irritate your flock's respiratory system if they roost on the floor.

Joint swelling and loss of feathers are just two of the side effects this can have on their bodies.

How to break the habit:

Lift the birds carefully onto the perch after dark to coax them into using it as a roost for the night. They will frequently abandon your efforts by just jumping back off. Adopting the new behavior may take a few days. To clean your backyard chicken coop, take out the cleaning tray before putting your chickens on the porch. Alternatively, make the platforms lower to the earth.

Bullying

Hens have been known to be cold to one another on occasion. The pecking order is something that develops naturally in all flocks. If some of your hens are being very rough with one another, to the point that they are harming one another or being completely excluded from the flock, you can follow the measures outlined below to try to lessen the severity of the situation.

Why is it important to stop?

If one of your chickens gets hurt, it could encourage the others to keep pecking at them, putting their lives in danger.

As a result of the other chickens' refusal to allow it near the food and water, an outcast hen may have very restricted access to these necessities. This raises the risk that they will become malnourished.

How to break the habit:

Separate the flock into two parts if things get really bad. They will likely rearrange themselves as a result, which will benefit the hen at the bottom of the pecking order.

To quickly treat any injured birds, separate them from the flock. This gives them a chance to rest and relax after a hard period of work.

The excluded hen will have a greater chance of getting the nutrition she needs if there are two sets of feeders and waterers.

Fighting Like a Bunch of Chickens Trying to Pick Each Other's Feathers

If chickens continue to pick at the feathers of their flock mates, it might spread disease.

Why is it important to stop?

If other chickens see blood, they may try to fix the problem by pecking at the injury, making it worse.

Chickens can get seriously hurt if their bad behavior is allowed to persist.

How to break the habit:

If a chicken gets hurt or loses feathers, it's best to keep it in quarantine until it heals. Don't let your chickens become bored; they may start picking at each other's feathers.

I would love to hear from you!

It's through your support and reviews that my book is able to reach the haands of other readres too. Please take 60 seconds to kindly leave a review on Amazon. Please scan the QR code below. If you reside in a country that isn't listed, please use the link provided in your Amazon order.

Please follow these simple steps to rate/review my book:

1. Open your camera on your phone
2. Hover it over the QR code below
3. Rate/review my book

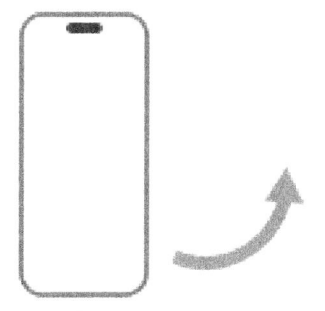

All it takes is 60 seconds to make a difference!

Conclusion

As you can see, there is a great deal involved in keeping hens in your own backyard. It is difficult to fathom life without chickens once you have owned a few, witnessed the hatching of your flock's chicks, tasted fresh eggs on a regular basis, and watched a hen chase a bug, leap into the air, and snag it. Chicken-keeping as a hobby is becoming increasingly common. There are a lot of cities where it's legal to maintain a chicken coop. There are several active Meetup groups and Backyard Chicken Clubs for anyone interested in keeping hens at home. In addition to being a terrific place to find help with the nuts and bolts of life, they are also a fantastic resource for more in-depth questions.

Hang around with other chicken-keepers. Raising hens in your backyard is easier than raising a dog, less expensive than buying exotic fish, and more rewarding than either of those things combined. Chickens are definitely among the greenest pets you could ever have. Raising hens in one's backyard won't contribute to the littering and commercialization that plague many urban areas. Instead, you'll benefit from fertile lawns, enriched compost, and delicious, healthy eggs. Because keeping a flock of backyard chickens is so simple, you'll have plenty of extra time to enjoy them for their own sake.

Thank you for taking the time to read my guide to keeping hens in your own backyard.

Resources

Wilke, L. (2020, November 3). *How To Choose The Right Chicken Coop Model.* Hobby Farms. https://www.hobbyfarms.com/choose-the-right-chicken-coop-model/#:%7E:text=The%20best%20coop%20size%20for,access%20to%20an%20outside%20run.

Coop, T. H. C. (2022, April 26). *How Much Room Do Chickens Need?* The Happy Chicken Coop. https://www.thehappychickencoop.com/how-much-room-do-chickens-need/

gardeneditor7. (2020, August 28). *What to Look for When Selecting the Best Chicken Coops for You in 2020.* Gardening Channel. https://www.gardeningchannel.com/selecting-chicken-coops/

Steele, L. (2021, January 28). *Selecting The Right Chicken Coop For Your Flock.* Farmers' Almanac. https://www.farmersalmanac.com/selecting-the-right-chicken-coop-for-your-flock-22185

This Is What to Know When Planning a Chicken Coop. (2022, February 16). The Spruce. https://www.thespruce.com/plan-and-build-your-chicken-coop-3016689

How to Pick the Right Chicken Coop – Mother Earth News(2021, January 16). Mother Earth News – The Original Guide To Living Wisely. https://www.motherearthnews.com/homesteading-and-livestock/how-to-pick-the-right-chicken-coop/

Omlet. (2020). *Choosing Your Chicken Coop | Chickens | Guide | Omlet UK*. https://www.omlet.co.uk/guide/chickens/choosing_your_chicken_coop/

Coops, B. C. (2020). *How To Pick The Perfect Chicken Coop Spot*. Backyard Chicken Coops. https://www.backyardchickencoops.com.au/blogs/learning-centre/how-to-pick-the-perfect-coop-spot

Wenger, E. (2022, January 5). *How to Choose the Right Chicken Coop Size [2022 Guide]*. The Hen House Collection. Retrieved 2020, from https://www.thehenhousecollection.com/blog/chicken-coop-size-guide/

Daily®, E. F. L. |. (2021, June 19). *Choosing the Best Location for your Backyard Chicken Coop*. Fresh Eggs DailyÂ®.Retrieved 2020, from https://www.fresheggsdaily.blog/2021/04/choosing-best-location-for-backyard.html

purinamills.com. (2022, March 7). *Choosing Chicken Breeds for Your Flock| Purina Animal Nutrition*. Retrieved 2020, from https://www.purinamills.com/chicken-feed/education/detail/choosing-chicken-breeds-a-guide-to-different-types-of-chickens

Raising Chickens 101: Choosing the Right Chicken Breeds. (2020). Almanac.Com. Retrieved 2020, from https://www.almanac.com/raising-chickens-101-choosing-chicken-breeds

McNamara, E. (2022, March 20). *A quick guide on how to choose a chicken breed*. Chickencoach. https://chickencoach.com/blogs/learn/choosing-your-breed-of-chicken

McKenzie, C. C. (2020, April 10). *9 Chicken Breeds You Should Know*. Country Living. https://www.countryliving.com/life/g32097528/chicken-breeds-types/

Chicken Breeds | Choosing The Breed Of Chicken. (2020). Jane. Retrieved 2020, from https://www.chickencoopsdirect.com/free-guide/chicken-breeds.htm

Chicken Breed Selection. (2020). Ohioline.

Retrieved 2020, from https://ohioline.osu.edu/factsheet/anr-60

Farm, K. M. O. L. A. (2019, August 25). *How to Choose Backyard Chicken Breeds*. Pete and Gerry's Organic Eggs.https://www.peteandgerrys.com/blog/how-to-choose-backyard-chicken-breeds

BIlaniwskyj-Zarins, T. (2021, December 5). *Chicken Breeds Chart: Choosing Your Backyard Chickens*.Pip☒Magazine - Sustainability and Permaculture.https://pipmagazine.com.au/grow/chicken-breeds-chart/

Thurmon, A. (2022, March 4). *How to Choose the Best Backyard Chicken Breeds That are Perfect for Your Family*. Azure Farm. https://www.azurefarm-life.com/farm-blog/how-to-choose-the-best-backyard-chicken-breeds

Manion, B. J., & Ludlow, R. T. (2016, March 27). *Water Food and Treats for Your FreeRange Chickens Article*. Dummies. https://www.dummies.com/article/home-auto-hobbies/hobby-farming/chickens/water-food-and-treats-for-your-free-range-chickens-204280/

Omlet. (2020). *Feeding And Watering Your Chickens | Chicken Care | Chickens | Guide*. Retrieved 2020, from https://www.omlet.co.uk/guide/chickens/chicken_care/feeding/

Fisheries, A. A. (2019, May 13). *Poultry feed, nutrition and water*. Business Queensland. https://www.business.qld.gov.au/industries/farms-fishing-forestry/agriculture/livestock/poultry/diseases-health-management/maintaining-healthy-flock/feed-water

Coop, T. H. C. (2022, May 16). *Chapter Four: Providing Your Chickens With Water During Winter.* The Happy Chicken Coop.https://www.thehappychickencoop.com/the-definitive-guide-to-keeping-chickens-in-winter-chapter-four/

Can Providing Feed and Water on Hatching Improve Chick Health? (2020). The Poultry Site. https://www.thepoultrysite.com/articles/can-providing-feed-and-water-on-hatching-improve-chick-health

Lesley, C., Lesley, C., Lesley, C., & Lesley, C. (2021, January 25). *The Complete Guide To Chickens And Water | Chickens And More.* Chickens and More. https://www.chickensandmore.com/chickens-and-water/

Watering Backyard Chickens. (2022, March 17). The Spruce. https://www.thespruce.com/water-your-chickens-3016561

Stewart-Brown, B. (2022, July 29). *Management of Laying Chickens.* MSD Veterinary Manual. https://www.msdvetmanual.com/poultry/nutrition-and-management-poultry/management-of-laying-chickens

Management of egg producing hens. (2020). Mississippi State University Extension Service. http://extension.msstate.edu/content/management-egg-producing-hens

Laying hen breeds commercial management guide. (2020). Laying Hens. https://layinghens.hendrix-genetics.com/en/news/laying-hens-management-guide-alternative-systems/

Management | Insight on light. (2020). Laying Hens. https://layinghens.hendrix-genetics.com/en/articles/insight-light/

Egg production: How to manage need-based feeding of laying hens with amacs and split feeding control. (2020). The Poultry Site. https://www.thepoultrysite.com/articles/egg-production-how-to-manage-need-based-feeding-of-laying-hens-with-amacs-and-split-feeding-control

Limited, G. A. P. (2019, March 30). *Layer Poultry Farming Guide For Beginners.* Growel Agrovet. https://www.growelagrovet.com/layer-poultry-farming/

Common Chicken Health Problems. (2020). Almanac.Com. https://www.almanac.com/common-chicken-health-problems

Coops, B. C. (2020). *5 Most Common Chicken Health Problems.* Backyard Chicken Coops. https://www.backyardchickencoops.com.au/blogs/the-chookcoop/chicken-health-illness-diseases

Caring Pets. (2021, July 18). *Backyard Chicken Health Issues: Symptoms Treatment & Prevention.* https://www.caringpets.org/how-to-take-care-of-a-backyard-chicken-hen/health-issues/

Arnold, I. (2022, April 30). *Chicken Diseases and Health Problems.* PetHelpful. https://pethelpful.com/farm-pets/Chicken-Health-Problems

Gauthier, J., & Ludlow, R. (2022, April 27). *Chicken Health For Dummies Cheat Sheet Article.* Dummies. https://www.dummies.com/article/home-auto-hobbies/hobby-farming/chickens/chicken-health-for-dummies-cheat-sheet-208124/

Common problems and treatment methods for backyard chickens. (2020, December 14). Poultry Hub Australia. https://www.poultryhub.org/all-about-poultry/backyard-poultry/common-problems-and-treatment-methods-for-backyard-chickens

Poindexter, J. (2020, July 27). *13 Common Chicken Diseases Every Chicken Keeper Should Know About (and How to Treat Them).* MorningChores. https://morningchores.com/chicken-diseases/

Chicken health: how best to manage your flock's well-being. (2020). Raising Happy Chickens. https://www.raising-happy-chickens.com/chicken-health.html

Omlet. (2020). *Common Chicken Problems | Chicken Health | Chickens | Guide | Omlet UK*. https://www.omlet.co.uk/guide/chickens/chicken_health/common_chicken_problems/

Backyard Poultry | Healthy Pets, Healthy People | CDC. (2020). Janny. https://www.cdc.gov/healthy-pets/pets/farm-animals/backyard-poultry.html

Raising chickens for eggs. (2020). UMN Extension.https://extension.umn.edu/small-scale-poultry/raising-chickens-eggs

Keeping Chickens for Egg Production | Animal & Food Sciences. (2020). Linkon. https://afs.ca.uky.edu/poultry/keeping-chickens-egg-production

Trust, B. H. W. (2022, February 24). *How does my hen produce an egg every day? Find out here!* British Hen Welfare Trust. https://www.bhwt.org.uk/health-welfare/how-does-my-hen-produce-an-egg-every-day/

Chicken Behavioral Problems – Mother Earth News(2020, August 4). Mother Earth News – The Original Guide To Living Wisely. https://www.motherearthnews.com/homesteading-and-livestock/chicken-behavioral-problems-zbcz1708/

Chicken Behaviors: Dust Bathing, Mating, Preening, and More. (2020). Alm anac.Com. https://www.almanac.com/chicken-behaviors-dust-bathing-mating-preening-and-more

R. (2022, July 27). *9 Secrets revealed about understanding chicken behavior.* Run Chicken. https://run-chicken.com/9-secrets-revealed-about-understanding-chicken-behavior/

Easy Chicken Care Tasks to Make Part of Your Routine. (2022, May 28). The Spruce. https://www.thespruce.com/daily-and-monthly-chicken-care-tasks-3016823

Raising Chickens 101: How to Get Started. (2020). Almanac.Com. https://www.almanac.com/raising-chickens-101-how-get-started

K. (2020, April 23). *Benefits of Raising Backyard Chickens.* Dogwood Pond Farms. https://www.dogwoodpondfarms.com/benefits-of-raising-backyard-chickens

Should You Get a Chicken for your Home? (2020). Green America. https://www.greenamerica.org/green-living/many-benefits-backyard-chickens#:%7E:text=As%20the%20Gidneys%20have%20learned,to%20local%2C%20sustainable%20food%20systems.

Morrison, Z. (2020, March 10). *6 "Bad" Chicken Habits to Watch For and How Stop Them.* The Permaculture Research Institute. https://www.permaculture-news.org/2020/02/18/6-bad-chicken-habits-to-watch-for-and-how-stop-them/

Chicken Behaviors: Dust Bathing, Mating, Preening, and More. (2020). Almanac.Com . https://www.almanac.com/chicken-behaviors-dust-bathing-mating-preening-and-more

Johnston, C. (2021, June 20). *How to Start Raising Backyard Chickens in 7 Simple Steps.* Wholefully. https://wholefully.com/how-to-start-raising-backyard-chickens-in-7-simple-steps/

Steele, L. (2021, February 8). *Raising Backyard Chickens For Beginners.* Farmers' Almanac. https://www.farmersalmanac.com/backyard-chickens-23988

NORMAL BEHAVIORS OF CHICKENS IN SMALL AND BACKYARD POULTRY FLOCKS – Small and backyard poultry. (2020). Laureal. https://poultry.extension.org/articles/poultry-behavior/normal-behaviors-of-chickens-in-small-and-backyard-poultry-flocks/

Printed in Great Britain
by Amazon